Hybrid Cloud Management with Red Hat CloudForms

Build, manage, and control an open hybrid cloud infrastructure using Red Hat CloudForms

Sangram Rath

PUBLISHING

BIRMINGHAM - MUMBAI

Hybrid Cloud Management with Red Hat CloudForms

First published: August 2015

Production reference: 1240815

Published by Packt Publishing Ltd.
Livery Place
35 Livery Street
Birmingham B3 2PB, UK.

ISBN 978-1-78528-357-4

www.packtpub.com

Credits

Author
Sangram Rath

Reviewers
Kyung Huh

Marcus Young

Commissioning Editor
Kartikey Pandey

Acquisition Editors
Kevin Colaco

Neha Nagwekar

Content Development Editor
Shweta Pant

Technical Editor
Utkarsha S. Kadam

Copy Editor
Vikrant Phadke

Project Coordinator
Shipra Chawhan

Proofreader
Safis Editing

Indexer
Rekha Nair

Graphics
Jason Monteiro

Production Coordinator
Aparna Bhagat

Cover Work
Aparna Bhagat

About the Author

Sangram Rath is a Co-founder and cloud architect at Voverc and has 10 years of IT experience, primarily in the cloud computing and virtualization domains. He is also a freelance consultant and trainer and works on delivering solutions and trainings on OpenStack, Microsoft Azure, and AWS. In the past, he has worked for companies such as Hewlett-Packard, Microland, Mphasis, Bristlecone, and a start-up called CloudThat Technologies.

He took his first computer lesson at the age of 6 and knew that this was where he wanted to head. Sangram has a bachelor's degree in computer applications from Bangalore University and many technical certifications, such as Mirantis Certified Administrator on OpenStack; Microsoft Certified Solutions Developer: Azure Solutions Architect, AWS Certified Solutions Architect, VMware Certified Professional; and many more to his credit.

He is an avid reader and a foodie. He loves traveling and capturing moments through a lens. When he's not working, he loves spending time with his pet Labrador, Junior, in his hometown of Jeypore, Odisha, India.

I would like to thank my family and friends for the support and encouragement.

About the Reviewers

Kyung Huh is a senior consultant at Red Hat and is based in Korea. He has been working with Linux and open source software for more than 15 years as an instructor and a consultant. He has a lot of experience in implementing virtualization and cloud infrastructures such as Red Hat Enterprise Virtualization and Red Hat OpenStack Platform on the field.

Marcus Young recently graduated with a degree in computer science and mathematics. Then he got involved in system administration and DevOps. He currently works in software automation using open source tools and technologies. His hobbies include playing ice hockey and homebrewing beer. He also enjoys hardware projects based on microcontrollers and single-board computers.

He has written *Implementing Cloud Design Patterns for AWS, Packt Publishing*.

www.PacktPub.com

Support files, eBooks, discount offers, and more

For support files and downloads related to your book, please visit www.PacktPub.com.

Did you know that Packt offers eBook versions of every book published, with PDF and ePub files available? You can upgrade to the eBook version at www.PacktPub.com and as a print book customer, you are entitled to a discount on the eBook copy. Get in touch with us at service@packtpub.com for more details.

At www.PacktPub.com, you can also read a collection of free technical articles, sign up for a range of free newsletters and receive exclusive discounts and offers on Packt books and eBooks.

https://www2.packtpub.com/books/subscription/packtlib

Do you need instant solutions to your IT questions? PacktLib is Packt's online digital book library. Here, you can search, access, and read Packt's entire library of books.

Why subscribe?

- Fully searchable across every book published by Packt
- Copy and paste, print, and bookmark content
- On demand and accessible via a web browser

Free access for Packt account holders

If you have an account with Packt at www.PacktPub.com, you can use this to access PacktLib today and view 9 entirely free books. Simply use your login credentials for immediate access.

Table of Contents

Preface

Cloud adoption has grown by leaps and bounds in the last few years and so have the challenges in managing different cloud providers and the existing virtualized infrastructure. Enterprises end up managing these environments separately, causing management and cost overhead.

In comes Red Hat CloudForms, a unified management platform for both your cloud and virtual infrastructures. Red Hat CloudForms is built using the open source project ManageIQ, and is packed with added capabilities and enterprise benefits that Red Hat provides, such as subscriptions, updates, and support.

Red Hat CloudForms supplements your existing infrastructure—which consists of Red Hat Enterprise Linux OpenStack, Red Hat Enterprise Virtualization, and VMware vSphere—with advanced management and automation capabilities, chargeback, life cycle management, control and governance, capacity planning, and optimization. It also supports public cloud infrastructures, such as Amazon EC2.

In this book, we will explore its architecture, components, and feature sets. You will learn how to install and configure Red Hat CloudForms, build a hybrid cloud environment, and use the individual features. By the end, you should have practical knowledge of how to work with Red Hat CloudForms.

What this book covers

Chapter 1, *Red Hat CloudForms Internals*, highlights some of the challenges faced in managing a hybrid cloud environment, introduces Red Hat CloudForms, and provides information about its architecture, components, and features. They provide a unified management platform.

Chapter 2, Installing Red Hat CloudForms on Red Hat OpenStack, shows you how to deploy CloudForms in a Red Hat Enterprise Linux OpenStack environment as an instance; perform initial configuration tasks, such as setting the hostname, network parameters, and time zone; set up an internal PostgreSQL database; and start the management engine process.

Chapter 3, Building a Hybrid Cloud Environment Using Red Hat CloudForms, explains how to build a hybrid cloud by adding providers and viewing and editing provider information after adding. We also take a look at provisioning dialogs, which are used to raise a provisioning request.

Chapter 4, Provisioning Instances Using Red Hat CloudForms, outlines the steps to provision an instance into Amazon EC2 and OpenStack from the CloudForms web console. This chapter also introduces service catalogs. These can also be used to provision instances and virtual machines.

Chapter 5, Life Cycle Management Using Red Hat CloudForms, explores one of the key features of Red Hat CloudForms — life cycle management. In this chapter, you learn about the different stages of life cycle management, that is, request, approval, and retirement.

Chapter 6, Automation Using Red Hat CloudForms, talks about the automate model of Red Hat CloudForms, its hierarchy, and creating organization units such as domains, namespaces, classes, and instances. Here, you also learn how to create and invoke methods in automation.

Chapter 7, Managing Red Hat CloudForms, shows you how to control and govern the installation of Red Hat CloudForms and the hybrid cloud infrastructure using policies. We cover different types of policies and see how to take automated actions based on events and conditions.

Chapter 8, Monitoring a Hybrid Cloud Infrastructure Using Red Hat CloudForms, highlights the Insight feature set of Red Hat CloudForms. In this chapter, you learn how to view information about the hybrid cloud using the cloud intelligence dashboard, work with reports, collect usage metrics from virtual machines, use chargeback for billing and metering, and use alerts and the SmartState analysis.

Chapter 9, Optimizing Using Red Hat CloudForms, covers another key feature of Red Hat CloudForms, which is the optimization of the hybrid cloud. This chapter focuses on how to perform capacity planning of the virtual infrastructure by collecting and analyzing capacity and utilization data, creating charts of the data, and viewing the utilization trends.

Chapter 10, APIs for Red Hat CloudForms, introduces the two supported APIs in Red Hat CloudForms, that is, the REST API and the SOAP API.

What you need for this book

To be able to perform the steps in this book, you will need access to the Red Hat CloudForms Management Engine OpenStack Virtual Appliance, which can be downloaded from `https://access.redhat.com/` if you have a subscription. Although the examples in this book use the OpenStack version of the CloudForms Management Engine Appliance, other versions, such as the ones available for Red Hat Enterprise Virtualization and VMware vSphere, can also be used to install Red Hat CloudForms.

Alternatively, you can also use the open source version, called ManageIQ. However, certain features may or may not work. ManageIQ can be downloaded from `http://manageiq.org/download/`.

You will also, of course, need admin (or root) access to an OpenStack environment or a virtualized environment, such as Red Hat Enterprise Virtualization or VMware vSphere, to be able to deploy the CloudForms appliance.

Some examples may have additional requirements, such as access to an Amazon Web Services account.

Who this book is for

This book is for CIOs and solution architects looking for a unified central management platform for their diverse set of cloud and virtual infrastructures, and cloud or system administrators wanting to learn how to implement and use Red Hat CloudForms in their IT environment. The book is also good for reference if you have already deployed Red Hat CloudForms or know something about it and wish to enhance your knowledge.

Throughout this book, non-Red Hat technologies such as Amazon EC2 and VMware vSphere have also been used, so some experience or an understanding of these technologies will be great.

Conventions

In this book, you will find a number of text styles that distinguish between different kinds of information. Here are some examples of these styles and an explanation of their meaning.

Code words in text, database table names, folder names, filenames, file extensions, pathnames, dummy URLs, user input, and Twitter handles are shown as follows: "We can include other contexts through the use of the `include` directive."

A block of code is set as follows:

```
{
  "version" : "1.1",
  "template_fields" : {
    "guid" : "529ed0d4-3c55-11e5-a8c5-fa163e52df6c"
  }
}
```

Any command-line input or output is written as follows:

```
# curl --user admin:smartvm -i -X GET -H "Accept: application/json"
http://localhost:3000/api/vms/1000000074058
```

New terms and **important words** are shown in bold. Words that you see on the screen, for example, in menus or dialog boxes, appear in the text like this: "Provisioning is also a life cycle management step, and hence the option is available under the **Lifecycle** button."

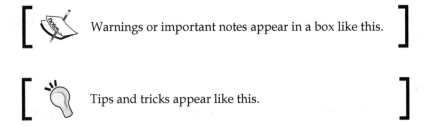

> Warnings or important notes appear in a box like this.

> Tips and tricks appear like this.

Reader feedback

Feedback from our readers is always welcome. Let us know what you think about this book—what you liked or disliked. Reader feedback is important for us as it helps us develop titles that you will really get the most out of.

To send us general feedback, simply e-mail feedback@packtpub.com, and mention the book's title in the subject of your message.

If there is a topic that you have expertise in and you are interested in either writing or contributing to a book, see our author guide at www.packtpub.com/authors.

Customer support

Now that you are the proud owner of a Packt book, we have a number of things to help you to get the most from your purchase.

Downloading the color images of this book

We also provide you with a PDF file that has color images of the screenshots/diagrams used in this book. The color images will help you better understand the changes in the output. You can download this file from `https://www.packtpub.com/sites/default/files/downloads/35740S.pdf`.

Errata

Although we have taken every care to ensure the accuracy of our content, mistakes do happen. If you find a mistake in one of our books—maybe a mistake in the text or the code—we would be grateful if you could report this to us. By doing so, you can save other readers from frustration and help us improve subsequent versions of this book. If you find any errata, please report them by visiting `http://www.packtpub.com/submit-errata`, selecting your book, clicking on the **Errata Submission Form** link, and entering the details of your errata. Once your errata are verified, your submission will be accepted and the errata will be uploaded to our website or added to any list of existing errata under the Errata section of that title.

To view the previously submitted errata, go to `https://www.packtpub.com/books/content/support` and enter the name of the book in the search field. The required information will appear under the **Errata** section.

Piracy

Piracy of copyrighted material on the Internet is an ongoing problem across all media. At Packt, we take the protection of our copyright and licenses very seriously. If you come across any illegal copies of our works in any form on the Internet, please provide us with the location address or website name immediately so that we can pursue a remedy.

Please contact us at `copyright@packtpub.com` with a link to the suspected pirated material.

We appreciate your help in protecting our authors and our ability to bring you valuable content.

Questions

If you have a problem with any aspect of this book, you can contact us at `questions@packtpub.com`, and we will do our best to address the problem.

1
Red Hat CloudForms Internals

This chapter highlights some of the challenges faced in managing hybrid cloud environments that contain a mix of private and public clouds and traditional virtualized infrastructure. It then introduces Red Hat CloudForms, its architecture, its components, and features that overcome these challenges.

The following topics are covered in this chapter:

- What is a cloud management platform?
- Hybrid cloud management challenges
- Introducing Red Hat CloudForms
- Architecture
- Components
- Capabilities
- Benefits
- Supported providers
- Types of provisioning
- The open source version of Red Hat CloudForms

At the time of writing this book, Red Hat CloudForms 3.1 is the latest version.

What is a cloud management platform?

Simply put, a cloud management platform is a piece of all-in-one software with integrated tools that provide a unified platform for provisioning, management, billing, control, and governance of resources across different types of cloud deployments, such as private and public, and virtualized infrastructures.

A more formal definition of a cloud management platform is well made by Gartner, which is a global research company in America.

Gartner defines a cloud management platform as:

> *Integrated products that provide for the management of public, private and hybrid cloud environments. The minimum requirements to be included in this category are products that incorporate self-service interfaces, provision system images, enable metering and billing, and provide for some degree of workload optimization through established policies. More-advanced offerings may also integrate with external enterprise management systems, include service catalogs, support the configuration of storage and network resources, allow for enhanced resource management via service governors and provide advanced monitoring for improved "guest" performance and availability.*

The source is http://www.gartner.com/it-glossary/cloud-management-platforms.

According to Gartner, when choosing a cloud management platform, here are some capabilities to look for:

- Self-service automated provisioning
- Chargeback
- Capacity management
- Performance management
- Configuration and change management
- Life cycle management
- The service catalog
- Orchestration
- External cloud connection

Hybrid cloud management challenges

One of the important challenges in running a cloud infrastructure is management. This challenge is compounded if you also have a heterogeneous environment of on-premise virtualized infrastructure. Let's take a look at some of the most common hybrid cloud management challenges companies face in day-to-day operations:

- **Centralized management**: Most companies will already have a virtualized infrastructure and also be using either both private and public clouds or at least one of them. Hence, they will have management tools for each of these infrastructures, for example, a management tool for VMware, another for a public cloud (such as Amazon Web Services), and then maybe a tool for managing a private cloud (such as OpenStack). The challenge is in managing them separately.

- **Life cycle management**: Life cycle management involves automation of tasks such as requesting resources, approval, provisioning, customization, reconfiguration, and finally retiring the resources. A lack of life cycle management capabilities can lead to losing track and continuing to run needless resources, causing management and cost overhead. This results from the need to manage individual silos.

- **Capacity management**: One of the reasons for which companies move to the cloud, especially a hybrid one, is to be able to meet the sudden demand of resources from a public cloud, such as **Amazon Web Services** (**AWS**). The challenge is to know when to cross over and provision new resources through automation.

- **Chargeback**: Being able to accurately collect utilization data and charge back a tenant or internal department is another challenge that most companies face. It involves performing a manual process or the use of a vendor-specific tool, which again results in manual aggregation in the case of a heterogeneous environment. Companies face the lack of a unified platform for chargeback.

- **Governance**: With self-service being one of the main reasons for cloud adaptability, governance becomes key to hassle-free, automated commissioning and decommissioning of resources. Also, in the case of a hybrid cloud, the challenge is to make it work seamlessly across environments instead of separate governance policies for virtual and the cloud.

- **Orchestration**: Orchestration templates are vendor-specific and fail to work across providers. The challenge is a platform from where an orchestration template will be able to deploy resources across virtual and cloud environments.

- **Integration**: A diverse IT environment consisting of physical, virtual, and cloud infrastructures running in different types of hardware, stack, and platform in different geographical locations makes integration of services difficult.

- **Security** and **Compliance**: This is a challenge that always figures at the top of the list. Administrators need to ensure that compliance is met when provisioning resources across different types of infrastructures, users do not have more than the required permissions, and resources are provisioned with a set standard or configuration.

- **Unified analytics**: Having a unified view of resources, their consumption across environments, and providers to monitor; viewing trends; checking performance; and forecasting are other challenges that businesses face with a hybrid cloud deployment.

- **External cloud**: Another challenge with hybrid cloud deployments is integration with external or public clouds for workload deployment. In most cases, this is managed separately in a manual way, or it is sometimes scripted, but still it requires a lot of hassles. Presenting external clouds as an extension of your data center or private cloud is still a challenge.

Introducing Red Hat CloudForms

Red Hat CloudForms is a scalable, open, and extensible management platform that provides insight, control, automation, and integration capabilities all under a single pane of glass. It is apt for managing resources distributed across private and hybrid clouds, and also includes support for traditional virtualized environments.

It can help you build a private cloud using existing virtualized infrastructure and deliver self-service infrastructure resources, such as compute, storage, and networking. It provides an advanced virtualization management platform with capabilities such as:

- Monitoring and tracking
- Capacity management and planning
- Resource usage and optimization
- Workload life cycle management
- Policies to govern access and usage

Red Hat CloudForms can also help you build and manage a hybrid cloud from a unified platform, or just provide enhanced management capabilities to existing private cloud environments built using platforms such as Red Hat Enterprise Linux OpenStack. Some of these capabilities include:

- A self-service portal and catalogs
- Controls for managing requests

- Quota enforcement and usage
- Chargeback and cost allocation
- Automated provisioning

It follows an open-hybrid cloud strategy, making it possible to use external technologies such as VMware, Hyper-V, and Amazon Web Services EC2 and run Linux, as well as Windows workloads alike.

The platform provides operational visibility and control across environments in a unified view using capabilities such as:

- Dashboards
- Reports
- Policies
- Alerts
- Approval workflows

Advantages

Red Hat CloudForms provides a host of advantages that provide a seamless management experience. Some of the highlights are as follows:

- An easy-to-deploy management appliance available for different virtualization and cloud platforms
- A lightweight web-based interface meant to administer, manage, and operate a private or hybrid cloud
- Directory integration support for control and compliance, which supports existing technologies such as Active Directory, IBM Blue Pages and LDAP
- A multitenant architecture that's secure and isolated, with each tenant containing its own data and network
- It provides secure and compliant management across infrastructure platforms by using policies
- Scalability
- It ensures high availability through the clustering of hosts and zoning of cloud resources
- Load balancing capabilities through clustering
- The unified management of resources spread across geographical locations

- Support for heterogeneous infrastructure and cloud platforms
- Improved automation through services and service catalogs
- A better optimization of resources
- A single tool to manage it all

Architecture

The architecture of Red Hat CloudForms consists of a host of features that together form the **adaptive management platform**, which sits on top of the virtualized and cloud infrastructures, providing a unified management experience.

The Red Hat CloudForms architecture; source: `http://redhat.com/`

The components of Red Hat CloudForms

Red Hat CloudForms consists of the CloudForms Management Engine, which is the primary component. This appliance is provided as a secure, high-performance, and preconfigured virtual machine in different formats for different deployment environments, such as **Open Virtualization Format (OVF)** for VMware, QCOW2 (QEMU Copy On Write) image for Red Hat OpenStack, and Red Hat Virtual Appliance for RHEV.

In addition to the CloudForms Management Engine, there are some other components that make up the platform:

- **CloudForms Management Engine Server**: This component is part of the CloudForms Management Engine Appliance and provides secure communication between SmartProxy and the virtual management database.

- **Virtual Management Database**: This collects information about the virtual infrastructure and appliance. It is usually part of the CloudForms Management Engine Appliance, but can be deployed on another machine as well.

- **CloudForms Management Engine Console**: This provides the **User Interface (UI)** required to view, manage, and control the CloudForms Management Engine Appliance. It uses Web 2.0 mash-ups and web service interfaces for communication.

- **SmartProxy**: This component can either be used as part of the CloudForms Management Engine Appliance or be installed separately on an ESX server. It performs actions on behalf of the CloudForms Management Engine Appliance on data stores. The communication between the appliance and SmartProxy takes place over HTTPS.

Capabilities

Red Hat CloudForms provides a lot of capabilities which can be broadly categorized into four different feature sets, that build upon one another to provide seamless, unified management of the hybrid cloud infrastructure:

- **Insight**: The insight feature set includes discovery, monitoring, utilization, performance, reporting, analytics, chargeback, and trending, which give operational visibility of the hybrid cloud environment

- **Control**: The control feature set includes security, compliance, alerting, policy-based resource access, and configuration enforcement, which provides control over the hybrid cloud environment

- **Automate**: This feature set contains IT processes, tasks and events, provisioning, workload management, and orchestration

- **Integrate**: This contains features such as systems management, tools and processes, event consoles, **Role-based Administration (RBA)**, and web services

Benefits

Red Hat CloudForms provides a host of infrastructure management benefits depending on the use case and implementation, some of which include:

- Flexibility in managing a heterogeneous environment from a single pane of glass
- Lower implementation and acquisition costs
- An open-hybrid cloud strategy
- A single tool to manage it all
- Quicker failover to the cloud
- Increased automation compared to vendor-specific tools
- Continuous optimization of resources

Supported providers

In Red Hat CloudForms, virtualization platforms and private or public cloud platforms are called **providers**. They are categorized as infrastructure providers and cloud providers.

Infrastructure providers

Infrastructure providers are platforms that provide virtualization capabilities to on-premise/co-located hardware consisting of machines that run a piece of virtualization software. Currently, the following infrastructure providers are supported:

- Red Hat Enterprise Virtualization Manager
- VMware vCenter
- Microsoft SCVMM

Cloud providers

Cloud providers are platforms or vendors that provide private or public cloud infrastructures with scalable computing, storage, and networking capabilities. The following is the list of currently supported cloud providers:

- OpenStack
- Amazon Web Services

Types of provisioning

Provisioning is the process of preparing, creating, or setting up a resource and making it available for use. This resource can be a virtual machine or a server in generic terms.

Red Hat CloudForms can provision virtual machines (also called as instances in the cloud terminology) and hosts (otherwise called servers).

Virtual machines

Virtual machines are provisioned from templates. The provisioning type (or where to provision from) varies from provider to provider.

The provisioning types supported on VMware are:

- NetApp
- VMware
- PXE

The provisioning sources supported on a Red Hat infrastructure are:

- ISO
- PXE
- Native clone

Instances

The term "instance" is used for virtual machines when creating in Amazon EC2 and OpenStack infrastructures. CloudForms uses images to deploy instances that are available from the respective cloud providers.

Hosts

Apart from the automated provisioning of virtual machines or instances, Red Hat CloudForms also supports provisioning of hosts using the Automation Engine server role and a template. The provisioning technologies supported are:

- PXE
- IPMI
- ISO (only from RHEV data stores)

The open source version of Red Hat CloudForms

There is an open source version of CloudForms available, called **ManageIQ**. Red Hat CloudForms is actually a downstream of this community product, to which Red Hat is a major contributor. More information about ManageIQ can be obtained from `http://manageiq.org/`.

Summary

In this chapter, we looked into the challenges that system administrators and DevOps personnel face in managing multiple environments spread across traditional virtualization and cloud platforms, and saw that the architecture and components of CloudForms have features that can solve this.

In a nutshell, Red Hat CloudForms is a heterogeneous cloud management platform that solves many operational challenges, not only for cloud infrastructures, but also for virtualized infrastructures from a unified platform. It addresses the capabilities that you should look for and much more.

In the next chapter, we will learn how to install and configure Red Hat CloudForms appliance on an OpenStack environment, access the browser-based user interface, and navigate around.

2
Installing Red Hat CloudForms on Red Hat OpenStack

This chapter takes you through the steps required to install, configure, and use Red Hat CloudForms on Red Hat Enterprise Linux OpenStack. However, you should be able to install it on OpenStack running on any other Linux distribution.

The following topics are covered in this chapter:

- System requirements
- Deploying the Red Hat CloudForms Management Engine appliance
- Configuring the appliance
- Accessing and navigating the CloudForms web console

At the time of writing this book, the *OpenStack Havana* release was used, so certain screenshots might differ based on the OpenStack release you are using.

System requirements

Installing the Red Hat CloudForms Management Engine Appliance requires an existing virtual or cloud infrastructure. The following are the latest supported platforms:

- OpenStack
- Red Hat Enterprise Virtualization
- VMware vSphere

The system requirements for installing CloudForms are different for different platforms. Since this book talks about installing it on OpenStack, we will see the system requirements for OpenStack.

You need a minimum of:

- Four VCPUs
- 6 GB RAM
- 45 GB disk space

The flavor we select to launch the CloudForms instance must meet or exceed the preceding requirements.

For a list of system requirements for other platforms, refer to the following links:

System requirements for Red Hat Enterprise Virtualization: `https://access.redhat.com/documentation/en-US/Red_Hat_CloudForms/3.1/html/Installing_CloudForms_on_Red_Hat_Enterprise_Virtualization/index.html`

System requirements for installing CloudForms on VMware vSphere: `https://access.redhat.com/documentation/en-US/Red_Hat_CloudForms/3.1/html/Installing_CloudForms_on_VMware_vSphere/index.html`

Additional OpenStack requirements

Before we can launch a CloudForms instance, we need to ensure that some additional requirements are met:

- **Security group**: Ensure that a rule is created to allow traffic on port 443 in the security group that will be used to launch the appliance.

- **Flavor**: Based on the system requirements for running the CloudForms appliance, we can either use an existing flavor, such as m1.large, or create a new flavor for the CloudForms Management Engine Appliance. To create a new flavor, click on the **Create Flavor** button under the **Flavor** option in **Admin** and fill in the required parameters, especially these three:
  - At least four VCPUs
  - At least 6144 MB of RAM
  - At least 45 GB of disk space

- **Key pair**: Although, at the VNC console, you can just use the default username and password to log in to the appliance, it is good to have access to a key pair as well, if required, for remote SSH.

Deploying the Red Hat CloudForms Management Engine Appliance

Now that we are aware of the resource and security requirements for Red Hat CloudForms, let's look at how to obtain a copy of the appliance and run it.

Obtaining the appliance

The CloudForms Management appliance for OpenStack can be downloaded from your Red Hat customer portal under the Red Hat CloudForms product page. You need access to a Red Hat CloudForms subscription to be able to do so. At the time of writing this book, the direct download link for this is `https://rhn.redhat.com/rhn/software/channel/downloads/Download.do?cid=20037`.

For more information on obtaining the subscription and appliance, or to request a trial, visit `http://www.redhat.com/en/technologies/cloud-computing/cloudforms`.

> **Note**
> If you are unable to get access to Red Hat CloudForms, ManageIQ (the open source version) can also be used for hands-on experience.

Creating the appliance image in OpenStack

Before launching the appliance, we need to create an image in OpenStack for the appliance, since OpenStack requires instances to be launched from an image.

You can create a new **Image** under **Project** with the following parameters (see the screenshot given for assistance):

1. Enter a name for the image.
2. Enter the image location in **Image Source** (HTTP URL).
3. Set the **Format** as QCOW2.
4. Optionally, set the **Minimum Disk** size.
5. Optionally, set **Minimum Ram**.

6. Make it **Public** if required and **Create An Image**.

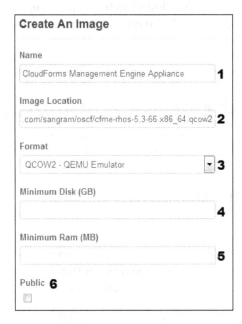

 Note that if you have a newer release of OpenStack, there may be some additional options, but the preceding are what need to be filled in—most importantly the download URL of the Red Hat CloudForms appliance.

Wait for the **Status** field to reflect as **Active** before launching the instance, as shown in this screenshot:

Launching the appliance instance

In OpenStack, under **Project**, select **Instances** and then click on **Launch Instance**. In the **Launch Instance** wizard enter the following instance information in the **Details** tab:

1. Select an **Availabilty Zone**.

2. Enter an **Instance Name**.

3. Select **Flavor**.

4. Set **Instance Count**.

5. Set **Instance Boot Source** as **Boot from image**.

6. Select **CloudForms Management Engine Appliance** under **Image Name**. The final result should appear similar to the following figure:

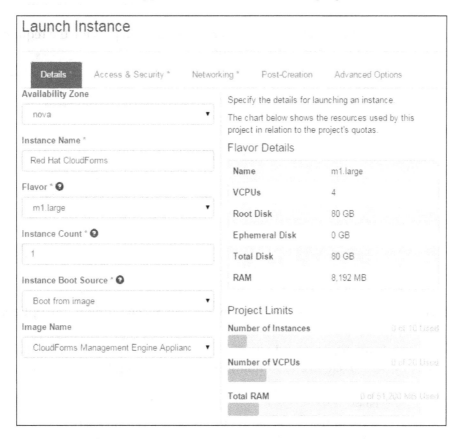

7. Under the **Access & Security** tab, ensure that the correct **Key Pair** and **Security Group** tab are selected, like this:

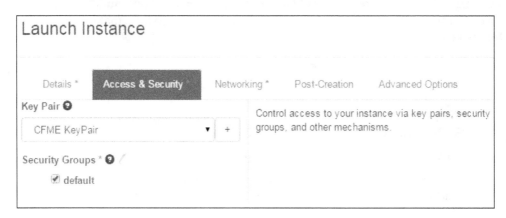

8. For **Networking**, select the proper networks that will provide the required IP addresses and routing, as shown here:

9. Other options, such as **Post-Creation** and **Advanced Options**, are optional and can be left blank.

10. Click on **Launch** when ready to start creating the instance. Wait for the instance state to change to Running before proceeding to the next step.

> **Note**
>
> If you are accessing the CloudForms Management Engine from the Internet, a Floating IP address needs to be associated with the instance. This can be done from Project, under **Access & Security** and then the **Floating IPs** tab.

Configuring the CloudForms Management Engine Virtual Appliance

Before we can log in to the dashboard and start using Red Hat CloudForms, we need to perform some initial configuration tasks to prepare the appliance for its operation:

1. Access the VNC console of the appliance from the OpenStack dashboard or remotely through SSH, and log in using the default username and password. The default username is admin and the password is smartvm.

```
CFME Virtual Appliance

To administer this appliance, browse to https://172.29.5.8
Username: admin
Password: *******_
```

 Note that if you've made a spelling mistake in entering the username or password, pressing *Backspace* or *Delete* won't help you correct it. Press *Enter* and it will prompt you to reenter the details.

On successful login, it will present a summary of the details, such as the hostname, IP address, DNS information, time zone, database details, EVM version, and EVM console's IP address. The EVM console's IP address reflecting here is usually the internal IP address of the instance and cannot be used to access the web console from the Internet:

```
Welcome to the CFME Virtual Appliance.

To modify the configuration, use a web browser to access the management page.

        Hostname:          host-192-168-1-2
        IP Address:        192.168.1.2
        Netmask:           255.255.255.0
        Gateway:           192.168.1.1
        Primary DNS:       192.168.1.3
        Secondary DNS:
        Search Order:      openstacklocal
        MAC Address:       FA:16:3E:94:49:D7
        Timezone:          America/New_York
        Local Database:    not running
        EVM Database:      postgresql @
        Database/Region:   vmdb_production / 0
        External Auth:     not configured
        EVM Version:       5.3.3.2
        EVM Console:       https://192.168.1.2
Note: Use the Ctrl-Alt-Del to exit out of any screen and return to the summary
screen.
You may need to use Ctrl-Alt-Ins to send a Ctrl-Alt-Del to the virtual machine.

Press any key to continue.
```

2. Press any key. It will take you to the **Advanced Setting** screen, which presents 17 different options to set up, configure, and manage the appliance. More options are available from the web console.

```
Advanced Setting

1) Set DHCP Network Configuration
2) Set Static Network Configuration
3) Test Network Configuration
4) Set Hostname
5) Set Timezone, Date, and Time
6) Restore Database From Backup
7) Setup Database Region
8) Configure Database
9) Extend Temporary Storage
10) Configure External Authentication (httpd)
11) Generate Custom Encryption Key
12) Stop EVM Server Processes
13) Start EVM Server Processes
14) Restart Appliance
15) Shut Down Appliance
16) Summary Information
17) Log Off

Choose the advanced setting:
```

The **Enterprise Virtualization Manager** (or **EVM**) server process needs to be started before the appliance can be accessed from the web console. Although configurations can be set up or changed from web console as well, it is recommended to set up at least the hostname, IP address, time zone, and database from the console before starting the EVM server process and accessing the appliance:

- **Network configuration**: In the **Advanced Setting** screen, select option 1 to set up **DHCP** or option 2 to set up a **Static** network configuration, depending on your choice.

- **Hostname**: Option 4 sets the hostname for the appliance. Set a new hostname if required.

- **Time zone, date**, and **time**: Type 5 and press *Enter* to set **Geographic Location**, **Timezone, Date**, and **Time**. Review and press *Y* to save the changes.

```
Date and Time Configuration

        Timezone area: Asia
        Timezone city: Calcutta
        Date:          2015-04-26
        Time:          20:24:00

Apply time and timezone configuration? (Y/N): Y_
```

Configuring the database

Configuring the database is the final step—and an important step—before we can start the EVM server process. The Red Hat CloudForms Management Engine appliance uses a PostgreSQL database. The following steps configure an internal database. However, an external PostgreSQL database can also be configured for use with the appliance. For more information on configuring an external PostgreSQL database refer to the online documentation at https://access.redhat. com/documentation/en-US/Red_Hat_CloudForms/3.1/html/Management_ Engine_5.3_Quick_Start_Guide/sect-Configuring_a_Database_for_ CloudForms_Management_Engine.html#Configuring_an_External_Database.

To begin with the database configuration, type 8 in the **Advanced Settings** screen and press *Enter*:

1. Set/create the encryption key, like this:

```
Configure Database

No encryption key found.
For migrations, copy encryption key from a hardened appliance.
For worker and multi-region setups, copy key from another appliance.
If this is your first appliance, just generate one now.

Encryption Key

1) Create key
2) Fetch key from remote machine

Choose the encryption key: |1| 1_
```

2. Choose a **Database location**, as shown here:

```
Database Location

1) Internal
2) External

Choose the database location: 1_
```

 If you are prompted for a confirmation, that is, **No partition found for database disk**. You probably want to add an unpartitioned disk and try again. **Are you sure you don't want to partition the database disk? (Y/N)**, select **Y**.

3. Set a database region number, as shown in the following screenshot:

```
Setup Database Region
Each database region number must be unique.
Enter the database region number: 1_
```

4. Set a password, like this:

```
Setup Database Region
Each database region number must be unique.
Enter the database region number: 1
Enter the database password on 127.0.0.1: ********_
```

5. A successful database configuration will print an output similar to the following figure:

```
Activating the configuration using the following settings...
Host:      127.0.0.1
Username: root
Database: vmdb_production
Region:    1

Initialize postgresql starting
Initialize postgresql complete
Create region starting
Create region complete

Configuration activated successfully.

Press any key to continue.
```

6. Press any key here to go back to the **Advanced Setting** menu.

Starting the EVM server process

The Enterprise Virtualization Manager or EVM server process is the root process that provides all the capabilities of Red Hat CloudForms, and it must be started before Red Hat CloudForms can be accessed and used.

To start the EVM server process, type **13** in the prompt and press *Enter*. Press *Y* to confirm. Post the successful start of the EVM process, the appliance is now ready to be accessed from a browser:

```
Start EVM Server Processes

Perform an EVM start? (Y/N): Y

Starting EVM...

Completed successfully.

Press any key to continue.
```

The Red Hat CloudForms web console

The web console provides a graphical user interface for working with the CloudForms Management Engine Appliance. The web console can be accessed from a browser on any machine that has network access to the CloudForms Management Engine server.

System requirements

The system requirements for accessing the Red Hat CloudForms web console are:

- A Windows, Linux, or Mac computer
- A modern browser, such as Mozilla Firefox, Google Chrome, and Internet Explorer 8 or above
- Adobe Flash Player 9 or above
- The CloudForms Management Engine Appliance must already be installed and activated in your enterprise environment

Accessing the Red Hat CloudForms Management Engine web console

Type the hostname or floating IP assigned to the instance prefixed by `https` in a supported browser to access the appliance. Enter default username as `admin` and the password as `smartvm` to log in to the appliance, as shown in this screenshot:

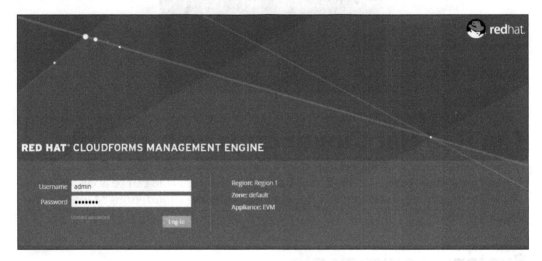

 You should log in to only one tab in each browser, as the console settings are saved for the active tab only. The CloudForms Management Engine also does not guarantee that the browser's **Back** button will produce the desired results. Use the breadcrumbs provided in the console.

Navigating the web console

The web console has a primary top-level menu that provides access to feature sets such as **Insight**, **Control**, and **Automate**, along with menus used to add infrastructure and cloud providers, create service catalogs and view or raise requests.

The secondary menu appears below the top primary menu, and its options change based on the primary menu option selected. In certain cases, a third-sublevel menu may also appear for additional options based on the selection in the secondary menu.

The feature sets available in Red Hat CloudForms are categorized under eight menu items:

- **Cloud Intelligence**: This provides a dashboard view of your hybrid cloud infrastructure for the selected parameters. Whatever is displayed here can be configured as a widget. It also provides additional insights into the hybrid cloud in the form of reports, chargeback configuration and information, timeline views, and an RSS feeds section.

- **Services**: This provides options for creating templates and service catalogs that help in provisioning multitier workloads across providers. It also lets you create and approve requests for these service catalogs.

- **Clouds**: This option in the top menu lets you add cloud providers; define availability zones; and create tenants, flavors, security groups, and instances.

- **Infrastructure**: This option, in a way similar to clouds, lets you add infrastructure providers; define clusters; view, discover, and add hosts; provision VMs; work with data stores and repositories; view requests; and configure the PXE.

- **Control**: This section lets you define compliance and control policies for the infrastructure providers using events, conditions, and actions based on the conditions. You can further combine these policies into policy profiles. Another important feature is alerting the administrators, which is configured from here. You can also simulate these policies, import and export them, and view logs.

- **Automate**: This menu option lets you manage life cycle tasks such as provisioning and retirement, and automation of resources. You can create provisioning dialogs to provision hosts and virtual machines and service dialogs to provision service catalogs. Dialog import/export, logs, and requests for automation are all managed from this menu option.

- **Optimize**: This menu option provides utilization, planning, and bottleneck summaries for the hybrid cloud environment. You can also generate reports for these individual metrics.

- **Configure**: Here, you can customize the look of the dashboard; view queued, running tasks and check errors and warnings for VMs and the UI. It let's you configure the CloudForms Management Engine appliance settings such as database, additional worker appliances, SmartProxy, and white labelling. One can also perform tasks maintenance tasks such as updates and manual modification of the CFME server configuration files.

Summary

In this chapter, we deployed the Red Hat CloudForms Management Engine Appliance in an OpenStack environment, and you learned where to configure the hostname, network settings, and time zone. We configured an internal PostgreSQL database and started the EVM server process. We then used the floating IP of the instance to access the appliance from a web browser, and you learned where the different feature sets are and how to navigate around.

In the next chapter, we will add infrastructure and cloud providers to build a hybrid cloud environment, and also see how to configure and discover resources already present in virtualized environments.

3
Building a Hybrid Cloud Environment Using Red Hat CloudForms

This chapter takes you through the steps required to set up a hybrid cloud environment using Red Hat CloudForms by adding different cloud and virtualization platforms.

The following topics are covered in this chapter:

- Adding cloud providers
- Adding infrastructure providers
- Viewing and editing provider information
- Auto-discovering providers
- Working with provisioning dialogs

Adding cloud providers

Before we can start managing a hybrid cloud infrastructure, we need to build it. We do that by adding supported providers. Let's begin by adding cloud providers first. A cloud provider is a classification used by Red Hat CloudForms for platforms or vendors that provide private or public cloud environments. The term used for virtual machines in cloud providers is **instances**.

For the purpose of this book, we will add both OpenStack and Amazon EC2 as examples. Currently, only these two types of cloud provider are supported.

Adding Amazon EC2 as a cloud provider

Amazon EC2 is a compute offering from Amazon Web Services that provides instances (otherwise called virtual machines) with CPU, memory, and some storage. Every region in Amazon Web Services is added as a separate cloud provider.

To begin, click on the **Clouds** menu option and select **Providers**. Next, click on the **Configuration** drop-down menu and select **Add a New Cloud Provider**, as shown in the following screenshot:

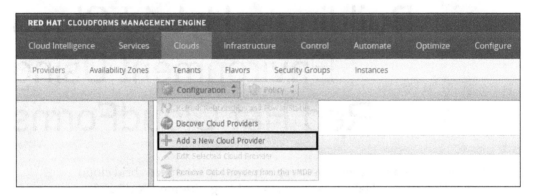

This will load the **Add New Cloud Provider** form. In the form, fill in the following details in the **Basic Information** and **Credentials** sections:

1. Add a name for the provider.
2. Select the type of cloud provider, which is **Amazon EC2** in this case.
3. Select the AWS region that you wish to manage.
4. Then select the Red Hat CloudForms **Zone** where you want to add this provider.
5. Enter the **Access Key ID** for the AWS account.
6. Enter the **Secret Access Key** and verify it.

> The **Access Key ID** and the **Secret Access Key** can be obtained/generated for a user from the AWS **Identity and Access Management (IAM)** console.

Once all the details are entered, click on the **Validate** button and ensure that the credential validation was successful, which is usually confirmed by a message at the top.

Finally, click on **Add** to add the Amazon EC2 region as a cloud provider.

Adding Red Hat OpenStack as a cloud provider

Although any OpenStack deployment (OpenStack installed on an Operating System other than Red Hat) can be added as a cloud provider, only Red Hat Enterprise Linux OpenStack platform deployments are certified to work and supported. Adding an OpenStack private cloud mainly requires the hostname of the controller node, IP address of the controller node and a root or admin credential of the OpenStack setup.

Follow the usual steps that were previously outlined to load the **Add New Cloud Provider** form. Fill in **Basic Information**, such as **Name**, **Provider Type** (which should be OpenStack), the OpenStack controller node, **Host Name**, **IP Address**, and the **API Port** number (the default is 5000).

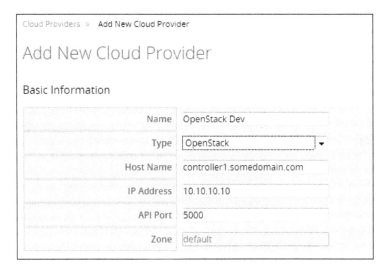

On the **Credentials** section, enter the **User ID** and **Password** required to connect to the controller node. These are usually the OpenStack dashboard admin tenant credentials. Click on **Validate** to ensure that the authentication is successful, as shown in the following screenshot:

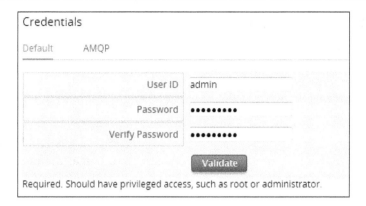

Additionally, if event handling is required, the credentials for the OpenStack AMQP messaging broker need to be provided as well.

 Advanced Message Queuing Protocol (AMQP), implemented using either RabbitMQ or Qpid, is a messaging technology used by OpenStack for decoupled communication between various internal components.

For example, if you are using RabbitMQ on a Red Hat server, you can retrieve the credentials from the /etc/rabbitmq/rabbitmq.config file.

Click on the **AMQP** tab, enter **User ID** and **Password**, and click on **Validate** to ensure successful authentication, as shown in this screenshot:

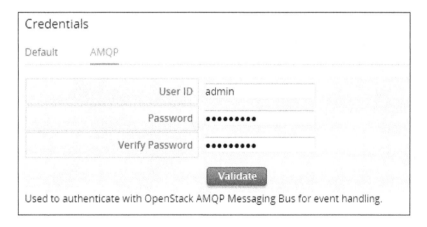

Finally, click on **Add** to add the Red Hat OpenStack private cloud as a cloud provider.

Adding infrastructure providers

An infrastructure provider is a classification used in Red Hat CloudForms for on-premise/colocated virtualized platforms, such as VMware and Red Hat Enterprise Virtualization, that provide virtual machines for consumption. Also, like cloud providers, before we can manage them, we need to add them to the CloudForms Management Engine Appliance.

Adding an infrastructure provider is a two-step process. First, we add the provider to the CloudForms Management Engine database, and then authenticate against all its hosts.

Adding VMware as an infrastructure provider

To begin, click on the **Infrastructure** menu option and select **Providers**. Next, click on the **Configuration** button and select **Add a New Infrastructure Provider**, like this:

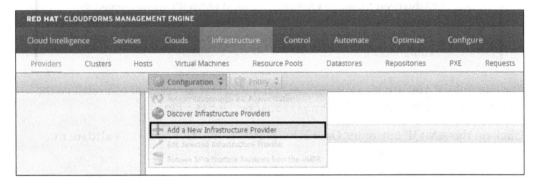

Similar to the case of adding a cloud provider, a form is presented, requesting **Basic Information**, such as **Name**, **Type** of **Infrastructure Provider**, **Host Name** and **IP Address**, and **Credentials**. For credentials, usually the `root` is set as the **User ID** and **Password** of the vCenter server need to be provided. Alternatively, another user ID that has administrative privilege can also be used.

Once all of the information is entered, click on **Validate** and ensure that the credential validation is successful, which is followed by a confirmation message. Then click on **Add** to finish adding the infrastructure provider, as shown in this screenshot:

Adding Red Hat Enterprise Virtualization as an infrastructure provider

To add a Red Hat Enterprise Virtualization setup as an infrastructure provider, select the provider **Type** as **Red Hat Enterprise Virtualization** on the **Add New Infrastructure Provider** form. Provide additional basic information, such as **Name**, **Host Name** (which is usually the server where Red Hat Enterprise Virtualization Manager is installed), **IP Address**, and **API Port**, and set the CloudForms **Zone**.

Next, provide the credentials to be used for authentication, such as **User ID** (usually admin@internal) and **Password**, as shown in this screenshot:

Additionally, if you wish to collect the historical **capacity and utilization (C & U)** data for Red Hat Enterprise Virtualization Manager, add the credentials for the Red Hat capacity and utilization database in the **C & U Database** tab. Capacity and utilization are covered in detail in *Chapter 9, Optimizing Using Red Hat CloudForms*.

Click on **Add** to add the Red Hat Enterprise Virtualization provider.

Authenticating infrastructure provider hosts

After adding an infrastructure provider, we must authenticate to all its physical hosts (or hypervisors) to be able to use CloudForms' capabilities on them. This applies only to infrastructure providers such as VMware, Red Hat Enterprise Virtualization, and Microsoft SCVMM.

To perform this step, select **Provider** (from the **Infrastructure Providers** summary screen), then click on **Hosts** in the **Relationships** section, display all the hosts of that provider, select all the hosts you wish to authenticate (or click on **Check All** if you are authenticating on all hosts), click on the **Configuration** button, and select **Edit Selected Hosts**. In the dialog that appears, enter the infrastructure provider admin credentials and click on **Save**. Depending on the infrastructure provider, additional information or credentials may be required.

If the authentication is successful, the **Authentication Status** section on the **Summary** page of that provider will show Valid and also a green tick mark in the provider thumbnail. We will see more about thumbnails in the next section.

Viewing and editing provider information

Once a provider is added, it is represented as a virtual thumbnail with four quadrants. Each quadrant provides some information about the provider:

- The bottom-left quadrant shows the icon of the provider that was added, for example, the AWS icon if the cloud provider type was Amazon EC2.

- The bottom-right quadrant shows the authentication status. It is a green check if the authentication is successful or valid, and a question mark or exclamation mark if the authentication is in process or invalid.

- The top-left quadrant shows the number of instances.

- The top-right quadrant shows the number of images.

An example in the case of the Amazon EC2 cloud provider type will be a thumbnail appearing like this:

Amazon EC2 cloud provider

Similarly, for a Red Hat Enterprise Linux OpenStack cloud provider, the thumbnail will appear as follows:

Red Hat OpenStack cloud provider

Clicking on a provider from the providers' list page loads the provider summary page which shows the **Properties**, **Authentication Status**, **Relationships**, and **Smart Management** information for that provider. The information displayed here changes from provider to provider.

To edit a provider, click on the **Configuration** button and select **Edit this Cloud Provider**.

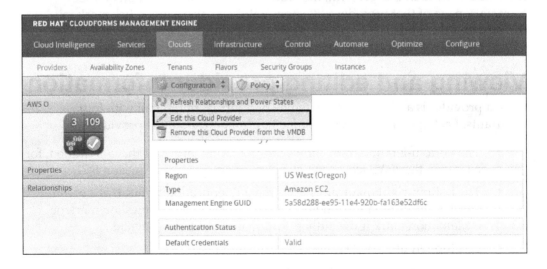

In the case of an infrastructure provider, the option will be **Edit this Infrastructure Provider**".

 Note that the provider type cannot be changed once it is set.

Auto-discovering providers

Red Hat CloudForms provides a way to auto-discover cloud and infrastructure providers. Let's look into both of them individually.

Discovering cloud providers

At the time of writing this book, only Amazon EC2 cloud providers could be discovered. To initiate a discovery, click on **Configuration** and then select **Discover Cloud Providers**, as shown in the following screenshot:

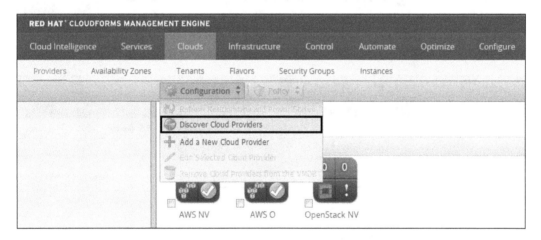

On the **Amazon Cloud Providers Discovery** page, provide your Amazon Web Services **User ID** and **Password**. These credentials are your primary Amazon account details, not **Access Key ID** and **Secret Access Key**. Click on **Start** for the CloudForms Management Engine to begin discovery and add the Amazon EC2 cloud providers associated with the Amazon account.

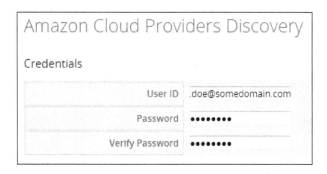

Discovering infrastructure providers

Similarly, to discover infrastructure providers, click on the **Infrastructure** menu and select **Providers**. Then click on **Configuration** and select **Discover Infrastructure Providers**, like this:

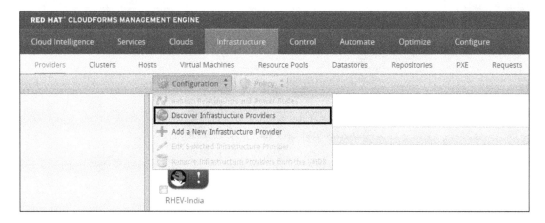

Red Hat CloudForms lets you discover virtualization providers from three vendors: Microsoft System Center VMM, Red Hat Enterprise Virtualization Manager, and VMware vCenter. On the page that loads, select the type of providers you want to discover by checking them, set **Subnet Range**, and click on **Start**. The CloudForms Management Engine Appliance will then try to scan those network subnets and add any infrastructure providers found.

Once the infrastructure providers are found, select the ones you want to add:

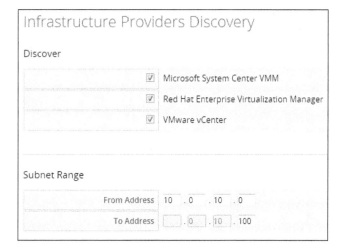

Working with provisioning dialogs

When provisioning a host or instance/virtual machine, a request needs to be submitted by filling in a provisioning dialog. It contains options and, in some cases, default values. Red Hat CloudForms provides a default set of such dialogs, but they can be customized as well.

Provisioning dialogs can be customized to mandate some required fields, remove or present certain fields and tabs, set default values, or create custom dialogs.

 You cannot edit default dialogs, and in a new dialog, you cannot add new fields or tabs.

Click on the **Automate** menu and select **Customization**. This will list four accordions, namely **Provisioning Dialogs**, **Service Dialogs**, **Buttons**, and **Import/Export**, which can be expand and collapsed.

In this chapter, we will only discuss **Provisioning Dialogs**. They are categorized into three folders, one each for host provisioning, virtual machine migration, and virtual machine/instance provision respectively. Clicking on one of them loads the default provisioning dialogs for it.

To view the provisioning dialog parameters, click on the dialog.

The structure of a provisioning dialog

To see how a provisioning dialog is structured and its contents, click on a provisioning dialog sample. This will load a new page showing basic information about the dialog and its content. The content consists of many lines of attributes and values that determine how the dialog is presented.

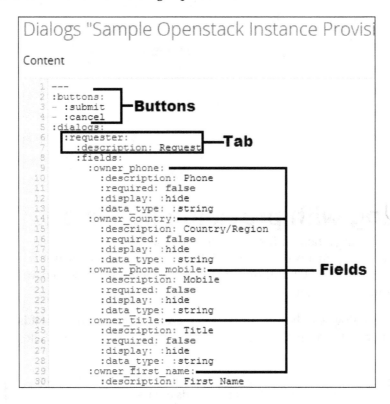

Let's take another look at the structure describing some more attributes, as shown in this screenshot:

```
Dialogs "Sample Openstack Instance Provis
104         :display:  :edit
105         :data_type:  :string
106      :display:  :show
107      :field_order:
108   :purpose:
109      :description:  Purpose
110      :fields:
111         :vm_tags:
112            :required_method:  :validate_tags
113            :description:  Tags
114            :required:  false  ── Required field or not
115            :options:
116               :include:  []
117               :order:  []
118               :single_select:  []
119               :exclude:  []
120            :display:  :edit  ── Field display status
121            :required_tags:  []
122            :data_type:  :integer
123         :display:  :show ──────── Tab display status
124         :field_order:
125      :environment:
126         :description:  Environment
127         :fields:
128            :placement_auto:
129               :values:
130                  false:  0      ─┐── Pre-determined values
131                  true:  1       ─┘
132               :description:  Choose Automatically
133               :required:  false
134               :display:  :edit
135               :default:  false── Default value if any
136               :data_type:  :boolean
137            :placement_availability_zone:
```

The display value for a tab is either ignore or show and for a field it is either edit or hide

Customizing or creating a new provisioning dialog

The default provisioning dialogs are not editable, so if you need to customize a default provisioning dialog or create a new provisioning dialog, you will have to start by copying a dialog. To do so, click on **Configuration** and select **Copy this Dialog**.

On the editing page, enter a new name for the dialog, fill in Description, and set the type of provisioning dialog. Then edit the content based on the requirements, making modifications to the attribute values. Once you are done, click on **Add** to finish.

Summary

In this chapter, you learned how to add or build a hybrid cloud environment by adding cloud and infrastructure providers. We also saw how to view providers and edit providers-related information. Then we took a look at provisioning dialogs that are required for raising requests to provision resources, their structure, and how to customize or create a new provisioning dialog.

In the next chapter, we will see how to provision resources such as virtual machines and instances. We will also take a look at catalogs.

4
Provisioning Instances Using Red Hat CloudForms

Now that you know how to build a hybrid cloud infrastructure by adding cloud and infrastructure providers, let's see how to provision resources in these providers from the Red Hat CloudForms Management Engine web console.

In this chapter, we will look into the steps required to provision instances in the Amazon EC2 and Red Hat Enterprise Linux OpenStack platform cloud providers. The steps for provisioning virtual machines as infrastructure providers are also similar.

The following topics are covered in this chapter:

- Images
- The provisioning process
- Provisioning an EC2 instance
- Provisioning an OpenStack instance
- Introduction to catalogs and service catalogs

Introduction to provisioning

Provisioning is the process of creating an instance or virtual machine from an image or template. Usually, provisioning of instances in a cloud environment (or virtual machines in a virtualized environment) involves logging in to the provider-specific management console or command-line tools. As discussed earlier, this is a challenge if you have different cloud/virtual providers, but CloudForms helps us overcome this through a unified management portal where we are able to provision instances or virtual machines from a central location.

Provisioning is also a life cycle management step, and hence the option is available under the **Lifecycle** button.

We provision an instance in a cloud provider or a virtual machine in an infrastructure provider, and the process involves three stages. They are:

- Request
- Approve
- Deploy

The information required in each of these steps varies depending on whether we are deploying an instance or a virtual machine. We will visit these steps in detail in the specific deployment examples later in this chapter.

Images

An instance is launched from an image, which is simply a virtual disk that contains a boot loader, a preinstalled operating system, a root user, permissions, and other standardized configurations. Different cloud providers support different formats for these images. For example, Amazon EC2 supports provisioning instances from Amazon Machine Images (or AMIs) only, which have an .ami extension, whereas the OpenStack platform supports a variety of image formats, such as QCOW2 and ISO, as well as Amazon's AMI.

To view all the images available, click on the **Cloud** menu option and select **Instances**. In the left pane, click on **Images** by **Provider**. By default, it will list all images by all the cloud providers. To view images from a specific cloud provider, click on one of the cloud provider on the left and then click on one of available images which will provide additional information about the image.

The following figure shows an example of an AWS WordPress image:

Provisioning an Amazon EC2 instance

Provisioning an Amazon EC2 instance from CloudForms involves providing information in seven different tabs in the **Provision Instances** form, and we begin with these three steps:

1. Click on the **Clouds** menu option and select **Instances**. This will list all existing instances by provider.

2. Click on **Lifecycle** and select **Provision Instances**, like this:

This will show the list of all the images available to select from, in this case all AMI images of Amazon Web Services in that region.

3. Select the image you wish to provision the instance from and click on **Continue**, as shown here:

This will load up the **Provision Instances** form we visited in the last chapter. The provisioning dialog contains seven different tabs, which we will explore and fill in the following sections.

 Note that any label that has a * sign next to it is a mandatory field to be filled in.

Request

The **Request** tab requires mandatory information, such as **E-mail**, **First Name**, and **Last Name**. It has optional information, such as **Notes**, and also a **Manager** section, where we can provide a name. Whatever information is requested here can be customized in the provisioning dialogs section, which was discussed in the earlier chapter.

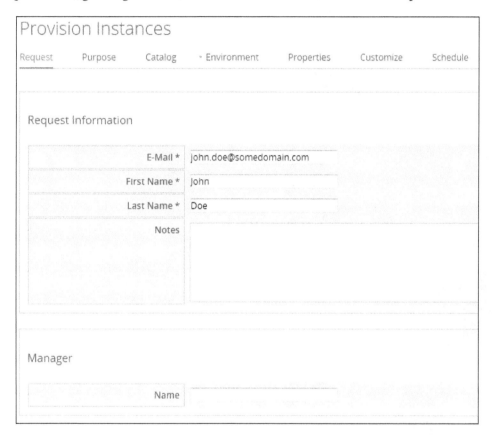

Purpose

In the purpose tab, we can select the **Tags** to apply for the instance. Tags can be helpful for easy searching for resources and categorization. They serve a useful purpose of resource identification later during monitoring or management.

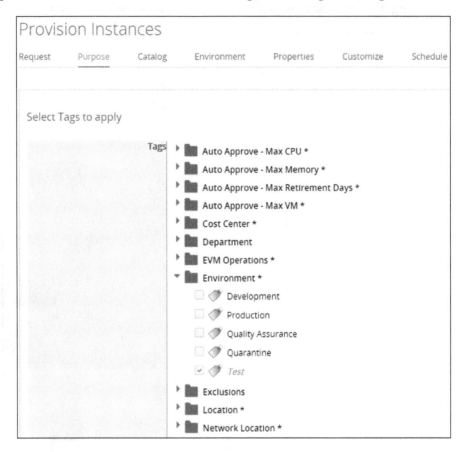

 Note that you can select only one tag at a time from the tag categories.

Catalog

The **Catalog** tab lets you set the **Number of Instances** to create from the image and specify **Instance Name** and optionally **Description**. You can also select an image from multiple options, if necessary.

Environment

In the **Environment** tab, you can choose additional instance placement configuration parameters, such as an availability zone, a virtual network, a network subnet, and the firewall rules and IP address to apply. The configurable parameters vary from provider to provider. You can also let the provider automatically place the instance.

Check **Choose Automatically** for automatic placement and uncheck to manually select the **Availability Zone**, **VPC**, **Cloud Subnet**, **Security Group**, and **Elastic IP Address** information.

For the purposes of this example, I will set it to **Choose Automatically**, which means that Amazon EC2 will automatically choose the preceding parameters for me, and this is usually the first availability zone, the default VPC and subnet, the default security group, and no elastic IP address.

Properties

The **Properties** tab requires that you set the **Instance Type** (or flavor) field, the **Key Pair** select a key pair for the **Guest Access Key Pair** field for remote SSH access, and the CloudWatch monitoring level.

 The instance type or flavor defines the attributes of the instance, such as the number of vCPUs, memory size, storage type, and so on as defined by the provider. For example, the `t1.micro` instance type in Amazon EC2 provides one vCPU and 613 MB memory.

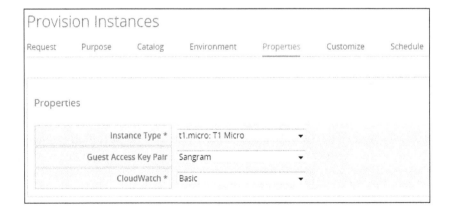

Customize

In this tab, you can set a **Root Password** for the instance, and other networking information, such as **Address Mode** (whether to get an IP through DHCP or static mode), **Host Name**, **Subnet Mask**, **Gateway**, **DNS**, and so on. None of the parameters are mandatory, however. So, for this example, I am going to leave the defaults and skip to the next tab.

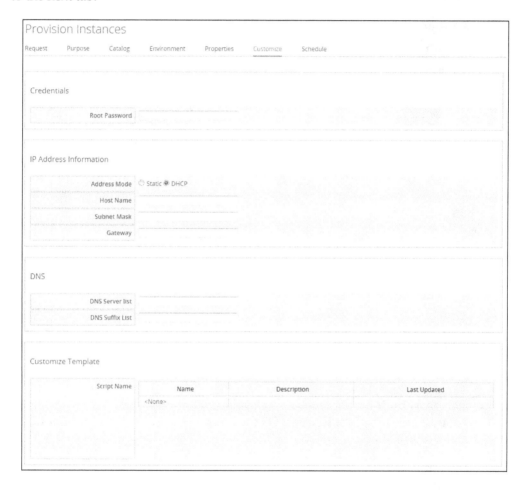

Schedule

The **Schedule** tab lets you set a **Schedule** (date and time) to launch the instance or **Immediately on Approval** In the **Schedule** tab one can choose to provision the instance Immediately on **Approval or Schedule** a specific data and time by selecting the **Schedule** radio button. You can also set the instance retirement time parameter called **Time until Retirement** from one of the following default options:

- Indefinite
- 1 month
- 3 months
- 6 months

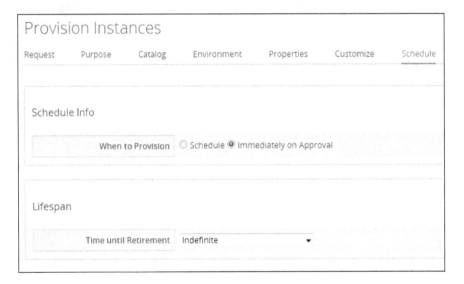

Finally, click on **Submit** for the request to be submitted for approval. At this point, Red Hat CloudForms assigns a **Request ID** for this request to track and troubleshoot in the event of a problem.

To view the status of the request, click on **Services** and select **Requests**. Then wait for the requested state to reflect as **Active** before starting to work with it.

Depending on the approval process, this can be an instant automatic approval or a manual one. In this example, since the request was made by an admin and it conforms to the auto-approval process (you will learn more about them in the next chapter), the approval will be automatic.

Once approved, CloudForms will initiate the deployment process and fulfill the request.

Provisioning an OpenStack instance

Provisioning an OpenStack instance is similar to the aforementioned set of steps, with the exception of a few fields and values that change due to a different cloud provider in question. An outline of the steps involved is as follows:

1. Select **Clouds** and then **Instances**.

2. Click on **Lifecycle** and select **Provision Instances**.

3. Select an existing OpenStack image from the list and click on **Continue**.

4. The default provisioning request dialog appears, with the **Request** tab highlighted. Fill in the following details on it:

   ◦ **Email Address**

   ◦ **First Name**

   ◦ **Last Name**

   ◦ **Notes** (optional)

   ◦ **Manager Name** (optional)

5. Select the **Purpose** tab and choose the desired **Tag** category.

6. In the **Catalog** tab:

   ◦ Ensure that the correct OpenStack **Image** is selected

   ◦ Set **Number of Instances** (optional; the default is **1**)

   ◦ Provide an **Instance Name**

   ◦ And provide an **Instance Description** (optional)

7. Select the **Environment** tab and choose the **Placement** mode. As we saw in the case of provisioning EC2 instances, to automatically place the instance in a provider selected environment, select the **Choose Automatically** checkbox. If choosing to set the instance environment manually, fill in the following options:

   ◦ **Tenant**

   ◦ **Availability Zone**

   ◦ **Cloud Network**

   ◦ **Security Groups**

   ◦ **Public IP Address**

8. In the **Properties** tab, set:

   ◦ **Instance Type**

   ◦ **Guest Access Key Pair** (optional)

9. Select the **Customize** tab and set the optional parameters, such as **Root Password**, **IP Address Information**, **DNS**, and **Customize Template** (if any).

10. Finally, in the **Schedule** tab, choose whether to provision **Immediately on Approval** or on **Schedule** and set a **Lifespan** option.

11. Click on **Submit** to initiate the provisioning request process and send for approval.

Catalogs and service catalogs

Catalogs are another way of provisioning a set of instances or virtual machines and are used to create application stacks that contain more than one instance or virtual machine. For example, let's consider a multi-tier web application that contains a web tier, an application tier and a database tier, and we want our stack to consist of two instances in each tier for high availability and failover. Instead of provisioning each instance manually, we can create a catalog that contains the entire deployment information, thus referred to a single template to provision the entire stack. When provisioning is enabled in a catalog, it is called a **service catalog**.

Catalog Items, **Catalogs**, and **Service Catalogs** are accessible from the **Catalogs** tab in the **Services** menu.

Summary

In this chapter, you learned how to provision instances from Red Hat CloudForms. Also, you were introduced to catalogs and service catalogs, which can be used to provision an entire multitier service with less effort.

In the next chapter, we will look further into provisioning requests and the instance life cycle.

5
Life Cycle Management Using Red Hat CloudForms

In this chapter, we will look a bit deeper into life cycle activities, such as request approval and retiring. We will also take a look at state machines and quotas, which play an important role in the life cycle management process.

The following topics will be covered in this chapter:

- Life cycle management
- State machines
- Viewing requests
- Automatic and manual approval of requests
- Retiring instances/virtual machines
- Modifying a state machine
- Quotas

Life cycle management

There are broadly two life cycle management activities that can be carried out for instances and virtual machines. They are as follows:

- **Provisioning**: This activity has three phases to it: request, approval, and provisioning (or creation) of the instance or virtual machine. You learned how to submit a provisioning request in the last chapter. In this chapter, we will focus on the approval phase.

- **Retirement**: This activity decides when the instance or virtual machine will be terminated.

State machines

A **state machine** is a collection of a number of states, where each state refers to a process that is happening and follows a cycle by transitioning from one state to another. Successful completion of the previous state is necessary for the next state to begin.

CloudForms includes some default state machines in the ManageIQ or CloudForms domain, which cannot be changed. **ProvisionRequestApproval** is one such state machine that we will work with in this chapter and it is relevant for the request approval process.

State machine components

There are six state machine components that you can work with and set values for:

- On_Entry: This component will run a desired method upon entering the state
- On_Exit: This component lets you run a method when exiting the state
- On_Error: This can run a method if there is an error during the running state
- Default value: This runs the desired method after the On_Entry method
- Max retries: This will retry the state a certain number of times before exiting
- Max time: This defines the number of seconds for which to retry the state before exiting

Viewing a state machine

As an example, let's see how the default **ProvisionRequestApproval** state machine looks in the ManageIQ domain.

To begin, click on the **Automate** menu option and select **Explorer**. From the left side, select **Datastore dominion** and navigate to **Datastore | ManageIQ (Locked) | Cloud | VM | Provisioning | State machines | ProvisionRequestApproval | Default**.

Clicking on **Default** will load the **default instance** of the **ProvisioningRequestApproval** state machine as shown in the following figure:

Name	Value	On Entry	On Exit	On Error	Collect	Max Retries	Max Time	Message
max_vms	1							create
ValidateRequest		validate_request		pending_request		100		create
ApproveRequest		approve_request				100		create

Automate Instance [Default - Updated 04/26/15 20:37:43 IST by system]

Fields

Viewing requests

Immediately after submitting a provisioning request, we are directed to the **Requests** page. You can also select the **Service** menu item and click on **Requests** to view all the requests (of a user), as shown here:

The **Requests** page shows all the requests and their current status. Requests can be filtered by different options, such as these:

- **Requester**: The person who submitted the request
- **Approval State**: This can be **Approved**, **Denied** or **Pending Approval**
- **Type**: This can be **All** or any one from the following list:
  - ° **Service Provision**
  - ° **Service Reconfigure**
  - ° **VM Clone**
  - ° **VM Migrate**
  - ° **VM Provision**
  - ° **VM Publish**
  - ° **VM Reconfigure**

- **Request Date**: You can see requests up to the last 30 days

- **Reason**: This field lets you additionally filter requests based on the reason for the provisioning request

The **Requests** page does not automatically refresh to show new requests or changes in statuses of existing requests. Hence, to update the requests page, we click on the **Reload** button at the top. The figure below shows the location of the Reload button and the different Filter By options available in the Requests page.

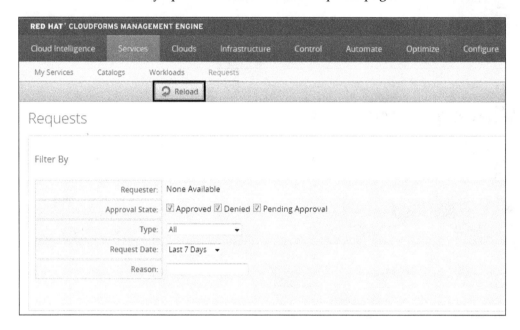

Approving requests

Requests for provisioning of resources can be approved primarily in two different ways: manually, from the Red Hat CloudForms Management Engine console, or automatically. Additionally, an external method of request approval can also be used. However, that is not in the scope of this book.

Request approvals are managed by the **ProvisionRequestApproval** state machine.

Automatic approval

If a provisioning request meets the criteria mentioned in the **ProvisionRequestApproval** state machine, it is automatically approved. This is what we saw in the provisioning example in the earlier chapter. The criteria and its maximum values can either be set as a global default or be defined for each template.

For example, the default instance of the **ProvisionRequestApproval** state machine is set to automatically approve the request if the maximum number of virtual machines requested is less than or equal to 1, which is defined by the **max_vms** parameter. It has a value of 1, as shown in the following screenshot:

Since our provisioning request was for one virtual machine, it was approved automatically.

Manual approval

The manual approval scenario comes to light if the number of virtual machines requested is greater than the value set in the state machine instance's **max_vms** parameter or if it is blank.

Let's take an example again and see how manual approval works. Let's submit a provisioning request again by following the same process outlined in the previous chapter but with one exception. Set **Number of Instances** to 2 in the **Catalog** tab of the **Provision Instances** dialog.

Once the request is submitted, we are redirected to the **Requests** page. Wait for a couple of minutes and reload the **Requests** page by clicking on the **Reload** button. Notice that this time the request is not automatically approved, with a reason: **Request was not auto-approved for the following reasons: (Requested VMs 2 limit is 1)**.

To approve the request, click on the request to load the **Request Details** page. Next, click on the check mark in the tool bar, as shown in the following screenshot. This will enable the **Reason** field for the approver to enter comments:

Enter a reason and click on **Submit**, as shown in this screenshot:

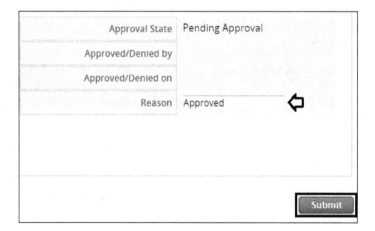

> **Note**
>
> A user needs to have the required permissions to approve or deny requests or make any modifications. In this example, the requestor and the approver are the same.

The request state now changes to **Queued** with a green check mark, and the request will follow the standard provisioning process to launch the instance. To refresh the status of the request, click on the **Reload** button.

To completely disable automatic approval, do not set a value for **max_vms**, or set it to -1.

Other request-related tasks

Apart from approving provisioning requests, there are additional tasks an administrator can perform with the requests. They are as follows:

- **Deny**: Click on a request and then clicking on the red **X** sign, along with a denial reason to reject the request

- **Copy**: Click on the **Copy** button after selecting the desired request to make a duplicate of the request

- **Edit**: This button lets you edit a specific provisioning request

- **Delete**: Selecting a request and clicking on this button deletes it

The buttons for these tasks are available in the toolbar on the **Requests** page, as shown in this screenshot:

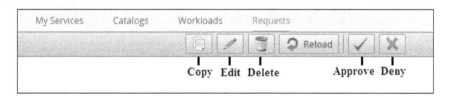

Some of these tasks may or may not be available depending on the user, type of approval, and so on. For example, edit and delete actions on a provisioning request can be performed only by the requestor and if the request has not been approved yet.

Retiring instances/virtual machines

The final step in the life cycle management process is the retirement of instances and virtual machines when their services are no longer required. Instances can be retired in two different ways:

1. By setting a retirement date:

   ○ During the provisioning request stage, by setting the time until **Retirement** field in the **Schedule** tab of the provisioning request form which is the last step during the requesting process.

○ After the instance is provisioned, by checking the instance and selecting **Set Retirement Date** under the **Lifecycle** button, as shown here:

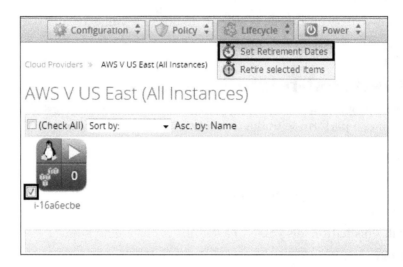

○ Enter **Retirement Date** and select when to send a **Retirement Warning** notification, as shown in the following screenshot. The options are **1 week before retirement**, **2 weeks before retirement**, and **30 days before retirement**.

2. By checking the required instance and selecting **Retire Selected Items** under the **Lifecycle** button, as shown in this screenshot:

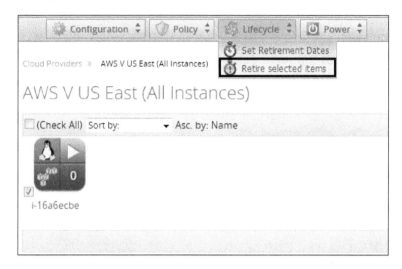

° Click on **OK** to confirm, like this:

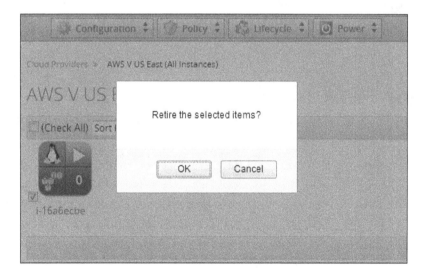

Modifying or removing the retirement date

Red Hat CloudForms also provides options to modify or remove a retirement date of a virtual machine or instance.

Click on the **Cloud** menu item, select **Instances**, and check the required instances. Click on the **Lifecycle** button and select **Set Retirement Date** again to load the Retire Vms settings page. The steps to remove or modify the retirement date is as follows:

- To remove the retirement date, click on the red **X** sign and then click on **Save**.
- To modify the retirement date, set a new retirement date. Don't forget to click on **Save**, as shown here:

Post-retirement scenarios

After the instances are retired, different policies can be enforced to ensure that they do not turn on again:

- Upon reaching the retirement date, instances or virtual machines are stopped even if they are in operation
- Retired virtual machines or instances are not started at all for a request coming from within CloudForms Management Engine
- Retired virtual machines/instances are stopped if the request comes from outside CloudForms Management Engine

Modifying a state machine

We saw earlier how certain state machines play an important part in the provisioning request approval phase. But these are the default state machines available in the ManageIQ locked domain. In a real-world scenario, the state machine parameters and values will be different as per the level of automation required.

CloudForms lets you modify these default state machines or create your own states in a state machine. However, since you cannot modify them in the default locked domains, you must create a user-defined domain, copy the state machine class to the new domain, and then modify them as per the requirements.

Let's take an example to see how this works. Here, we will consider the **ProvisionRequestApproval** state machine again.

Creating a new domain

The first step in modifying the state machine is to create a new user-defined domain. More details about domains are covered in later chapters of this book.

From the **Automate** menu item, select **Explorer**. Click on **Configuration** and select **Add a New Domain**, as shown here:

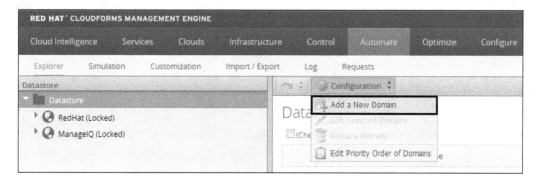

Fill in **Name** and **Description** and ensure that **Enabled** is checked, like this:

Copying the state machine instance

The next step is to copy an instance of the **ProvisionRequestApproval** state machine class to the new user-defined domain. You can copy the entire class or just an instance of it. In our example, the **ProvisionRequestApproval** class has only one instance, so we will go ahead and copy the entire class.

Navigate to **Datastore | ManageIQ (Locked) | Cloud | VM | Provisioning | State machines | ProvisionRequestApproval**. Check the **Default** class on the right-hand-side pane.

Next, click on **Configuration** and select **Copy selected Instances**, as shown in this screenshot:

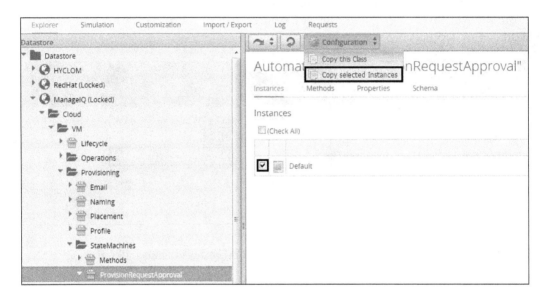

Since we have only one new domain for now, there is only that option available. Ensure that **Copy to same path** is checked and click on **Copy**, as shown here:

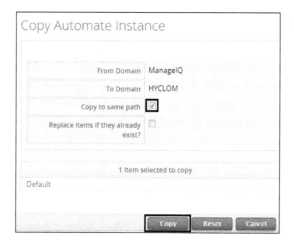

Modifying the state machine instance

Navigate to the new user-defined domain like this: **HYCLOM | Cloud | VM | Provisioning | StateMachines | ProvisionRequestApproval | Default**. Click on the **Configuration** button and select **Edit this instance**, as shown in the following screenshot:

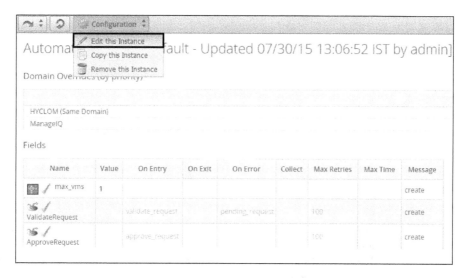

For this example, we will modify **max_vms** to **2**, as shown in the next screenshot. Click on **Save**:

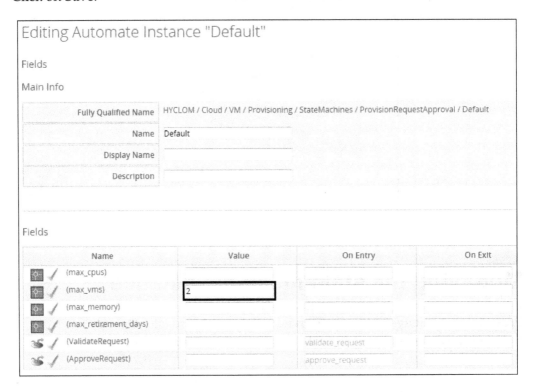

Other types of modifications

- To remove a state, clear the entries for all the components, such as **On_Entry**, **On_Exit**, **On_Error**, and so on

- To add a state, create a new field with a name and values for the components

- To modify a state, change the components' values to the desired values

Quotas

Once the provisioning requests are approved, before the actual provisioning of the instance or virtual machine begins, the Red Hat CloudForms engine checks whether the user or group has already used the maximum resources allowed. Again, the **ProvisionRequestQuotaVerification** state machine holds information about these quotas or maximum values defined in an Automate method.

As an example, let's view the default quota information for the ManageIQ locked domain. To do so, navigate to **ManageIQ (Locked) | Cloud\VM | Provisioning | StateMachines | ProvisionRequestQuotaVerification**.

Click on the **Default Instance**:

Automate Instance [Default - Updated 04/26/15 20:37:43 IST by system]									
Fields									
Name	Value	On Entry	On Exit	On Error	Collect	Max Retries	Max Time	Message
ValidateQuotas		validate_quotas		rejected		100		create

The method used to validate the quota threshold is `validate_quotas`, which is checked upon the entry of the state.

Modifying quotas

To modify the default quota, we must first copy the Default instance of this state machine to the new domain (as we saw earlier), then click on **Configuration**, then select **Edit this instance**, and finally make the modifications.

 To modify quotas, the user must be a super administrator or a user with administrative rights.

Summary

In this chapter, you learned what state machines are and how they are used in the life cycle process. We saw the different ways in which provisioning requests are approved and the different ways of working with requests. Also, you learned how to retire instances or virtual machines by setting retirement dates, which is the last step in life cycle management. Then we looked into quotas for provisioning.

In the next chapter, we will cover automation.

6
Automation Using Red Hat CloudForms

In this chapter, you will learn about the Automate model and how to create a custom domain, a namespace, a class, a schema, and instances of the class. We will also look into different methods that help with automation in CloudForms Management Engine and see how to invoke these methods using workflows.

The following topics are covered in this chapter:

- The CloudForms Management Engine Automate model
- Automate organization units
- Default locked domains
- Creating custom domains, namespaces, classes, schemas, and instances
- Methods of automation
- Workflows and how to invoke them

CloudForms Management Engine Automate

The CloudForms Management Engine Automate model provides real-time, bidirectional process integration by providing methods for automation, and uses an object-oriented hierarchy to control the automation functions.

The Automate organizational units

There are six organizational units arranged hierarchically that are used by the CloudForms Management Engine Automate model, as shown in this diagram:

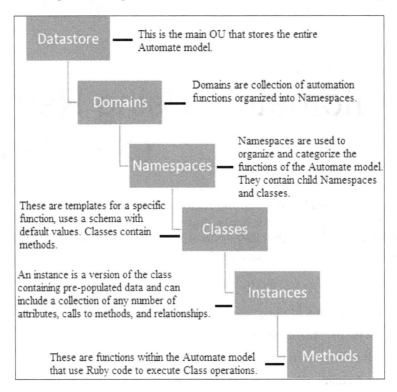

Domains

The CloudForms Management Engine appliance comes preconfigured with two locked domains:

- **ManageIQ**: This is the core domain of Management Engine and contains the following namespaces:
    - **Cloud namespace**: This contains methods and functions for cloud instance life cycle management operations, such as provisioning and retirement
    - **Infrastructure namespace**: This provides methods and functions for cluster operations, host provisioning, and virtual machine life cycle management activities

- ○ **Service namespace:** This provides methods for the service life cycle, provisioning, and retirement
- ○ **Control namespace**: This contains e-mail alerts for policy control
- ○ **System namespace**: This provides classes for automation activities

- **RedHat**: This default domain provides capabilities for advanced operations for Red Hat-supported cloud and infrastructure providers, such as Amazon EC2, Red Hat OpenStack, VMware, and so on. It has the following namespaces:

  - ○ **Cloud**: This provides methods and functions for Red Hat-supported cloud instances
  - ○ **Infrastructure**: This provides methods and functions for Red Hat-supported virtual machines
  - ○ **Integration**: This namespace is meant for talking to systems outside Management Engine, such as LDAP
  - ○ **Portfolio**: This namespace provides methods and a service provisioning template for Red Hat OpenShift
  - ○ **System**: This namespace contains the request class for OpenShift Enterprise

> Note that you cannot edit the classes and instances in these locked domains. But you can copy them to custom domains in order to use them as they are or to edit them. More details on how this can be done are discussed in the subsequent topics.

Working with the Automate model

The first step in working with the Automate model is to create a custom domain. We do this because changing any existing class or instance in the default domains may impact the overall functioning of CloudForms Management Engine, and also because some of the classes and instances cannot be modified.

> **Note**
>
> An "instance," with respect to the Automate model, is an instance of the class and not a cloud instance.

To work with the the Automate model, click on the **Automate** tab. This will load the **Explorer** pane by default (clicking on **Automate** and selecting **Explorer** also does the same thing). The options in the **Configuration** button change depending on what is selected in the left menu.

Creating a custom domain

To create a custom domain, click on the **Configuration** button and select **Add a New Domain**, as shown here:

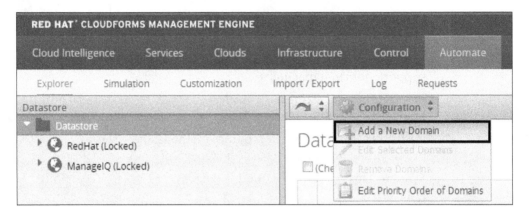

In the **Adding a new Automate Domain** dialog that appears, fill in **Name** and **Description** and enable the domain by selecting the **Enabled** checkbox. Click on **Add** to add the custom domain. In this example, I have named the new user-defined domain as HYCLOM, as shown in the following figure:

Creating a namespace

To create a namespace, select the new custom domain, click on the **Configuration** button, and select **Add a New Namespace**, as shown in this screenshot:

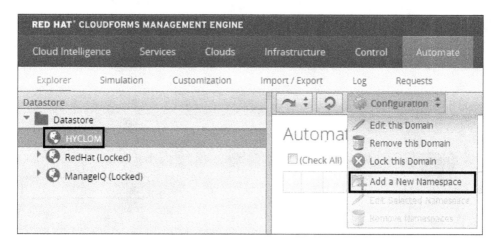

A dialog box will appear. Enter a name and a description, as shown in the following screenshot, and click on **Add**:

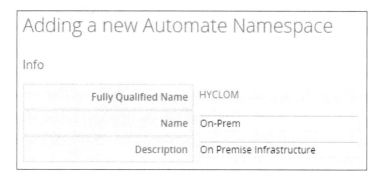

You can also create namespaces within a namespace.

Creating a class

Select the new custom domain and the desired namespace, click on the **Configuration** button, and select **Add a New Class**, as shown here:

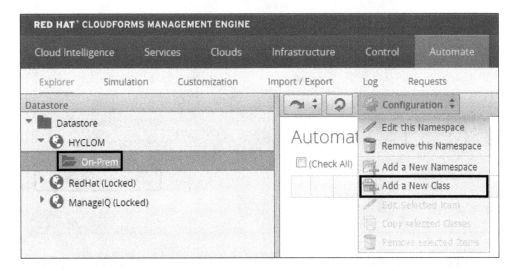

In the dialog box that appears, enter a name for the class under **Name**, a display name for the class in the **Display Name** field, and a description, as shown in the following screenshot. Then click on **Add** to create the class.

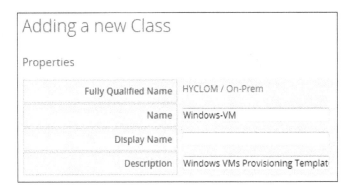

A class has a set of properties, a schema, instances, and methods.

Copying a class

In **Automate Explorer**, navigate to the desired class or instance in any domain. Click on **Configuration** and select **Copy this Class**, like this:

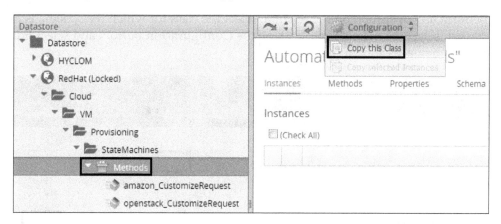

Choose which custom domain to copy it to (if there is only one custom domain, it is selected by default) in the **To Domain** dropdown, as shown in the following screenshot. If you wish to retain the same path as the source domain, leave **Copy to same path** checked. To copy to a different namespace, uncheck it and specify the path. Then click on **Copy**.

Note

Copying a class does not copy the instances in it. They need to be copied separately.

When copying classes across domains with the same path, the object overrides the class in **From Domain** if **To Domain** has a higher priority.

If you are selecting more than one class to copy, select the namespace that contains the classes, check the required classes, click on **Configuration**, and select **Copy selected Classes**.

Creating a schema

Now that we have a new class, we need to create a schema that consists of fields with attributes, methods, assertions, and relationships.

To perform any operation on the schema, select the class for which the schema is to be created, select the **Schema** tab, click on the **Configuration** button, and select **Edit selected Schema**, as shown here:

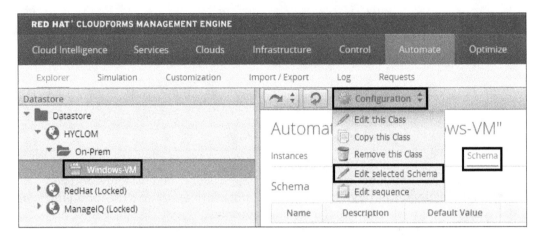

Adding a schema

To add a field, click on the green **+** sign. In the dialog box that appears, enter a name for the field. Then select **Type** (**Assertion**, **Attribute**, **Method**, **Relationship**, or **State**), **Data Type**, **Default Value** (if applicable), **Display Name**, and **Description**. Leave **Sub** (the substitution syntax of $ { }$) checked. **On Entry**, **On Exit**, **On Error**, **Max Retries**, and **Max Time** are required if you select the type as **State**. Otherwise, they can be left blank. Once all the necessary field values have been entered, click on the tick mark to create the schema, as shown in this screenshot:

Repeat for any additional required fields. Click on **Save** when done.

Editing and removing a schema

If a schema has existing fields, edit them as needed. Click on **Save** when done. The following figure shows an example of editing a class schema called Windows-VM, which we had created earlier:

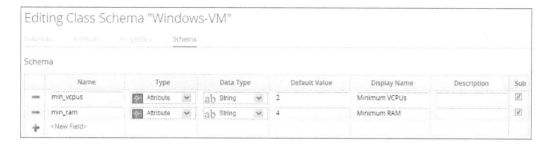

To remove the schema, click on the red - sign. Click on **Save** when you're done.

Reordering the schema sequence

Under the **Schema** tab, click on the **Configuration** button and select **Edit Sequence**. Select the field and use the **Move selected field up** and **Move selected field down** buttons to make the required changes. Click on **Save** when you're done.

Adding an instance

From the **Automate Explorer** pane, select the **Instances** tab. Click on **Configuration** and select **Add a New Instance**, as shown here:

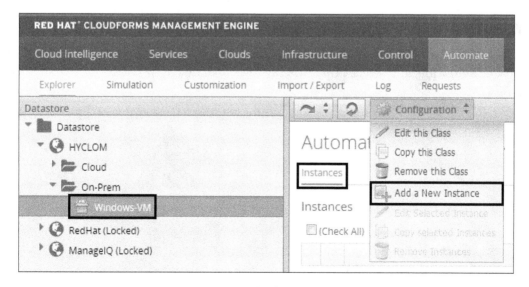

Fill in a **Name**, Display Name (this field is optional, and in this example, I have left it blank; if this field is left blank, the value in the **Name** field is used), and a **Description**, as shown in the following screenshot. Change the default class values for the fields, if required. Then click on **Add** to complete adding the instance.

Copying an instance

In the **Automate Explorer** pane, navigate to the desired instance in any domain, click on **Configuration**, and select **Copy this Instance**, like this:

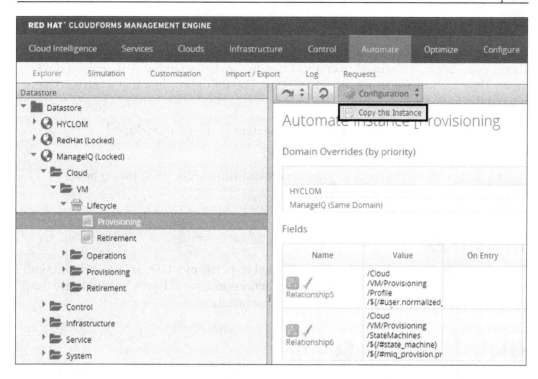

Choose the domain to copy the instance to in the **To Domain** dropdown (this dropdown is not available if there is only one custom domain). Choose whether you wish to retain the path or not by checking or unchecking **Copy to same path** (as in class). If an existing instance of the class is already present, select whether it needs to be replaced by checking Replace items if they already exist? check box. If left unchecked, the existing instance of the class is not replaced. Click on **Copy** when done.

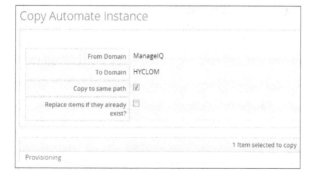

 Copying an instance creates the class if it's not present.

Relationships

Schemas for classes can be of different types, and the relationship type is one of them. Relationships are used to connect to other instances in the Automation data store. They are formed using the URI syntax. The following characters can also be passed through a relationship:

- Use # to set a message to send to the item in the relationship
- Use ? to pass an input to the method
- ${ }: This can be used to provide a substitution, the substitution being mentioned between the brackets

Methods

A method is a piece of **Ruby**-based code used to perform a task. It is associated with a class or an object. When creating custom actions and workflows, methods are used to manage objects such as virtual machines or instances.

Global variable $evm

A method, upon launch, has $evm, the global variable that allows the method to communicate with CloudForms Management Engine.

The $evm.root method is a root object in the workspace that provides access to the data that is currently loaded in the CloudForms Management Engine model.

Methods hierarchy

The CloudForms Management Engine Automate model's methods follow a hierarchy. At the top are the base methods, and then there are different levels and sublevels below them. Base methods and some other higher level methods, such as availability zones, providers, and requests, have additional methods.

For a complete list of the method hierarchy and the methods available for use, please refer to https://access.redhat.com/documentation/en-US/Red_Hat_CloudForms/3.1/html/Management_Engine_5.3_Methods_Available_for_Automation/index.html.

Creating a method

Apart from using the default methods available with CloudForms, you can also create custom methods or link to the existing methods using relationships. For creating your own methods, Windows PowerShell is also an option.

 To use Windows PowerShell to create methods and automation, install SmartProxy on a Windows machine with access to the Red Hat CloudForms Management Engine appliance.

Ensure you are in the **Automate Explorer** pane. To create a method, navigate to the class where you wish to create the method, click on the **Methods** tab, click on the **Configuration** button and select **Add a New Method**, as show in the following screenshot:

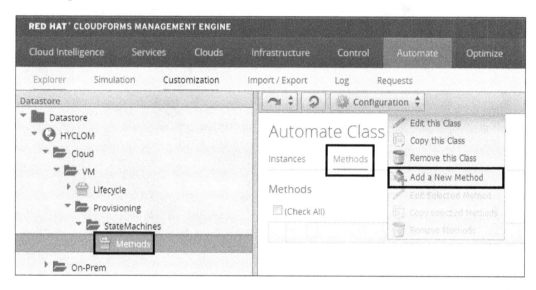

Fill in **Name** and, optionally, **Display Name**. Select **Location** as **inline** and then copy the script code to the Data field. For this example, I have copied the code from an existing method that can be found by going to **ManageIQ | Cloud | VM | Provisioning | StateMachines | Methods | check_provisioned**.

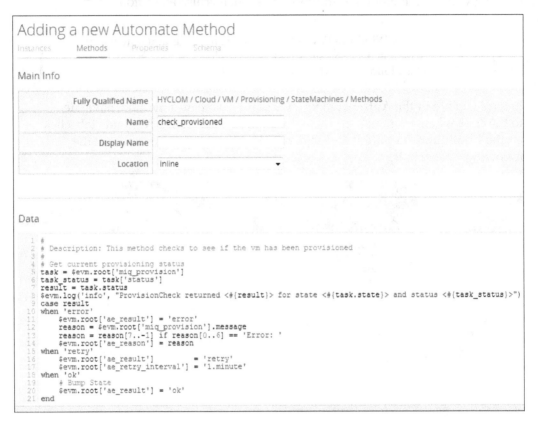

Click on **Validate** to ensure that the code syntax is correct and ensure that there is a successful response. Add any input parameters required and finally click on **Add**.

Automate workflows

There are four different ways in which workflows can be invoked in Automate:

- A custom button
- An event
- An alert
- A CloudForms Management Engine application

A workflow can be invoked using more than one (or all) of the preceding options. To understand this, let's look at an example where we need to create additional cloud instances in the case of a load. This creation of instances can be initiated by the following:

- An administrator who is monitoring the existing instances and sees that there is a spike
- An alert that shows that the CPU usage on the existing instance is more than 80 percent
- An existing instance that has crashed or is unresponsive

All invocations of an Automate model must enter through the `/System/Process` namespace.

Summary

In this chapter, you learned about the Automate model and its hierarchy. We saw how to create different organization units of the model, such as the domain, namespace, class, and instances. Also, you learned how to create methods for use in automation and how to invoke them.

In the next chapter, you will learn how to administer CloudForms Management Engine.

7
Managing Red Hat CloudForms

In this chapter, you will learn about the control part of Red Hat CloudForms, how to use policies and policy profiles to manage Red Hat CloudForms, and how to achieve automated actions based on events and conditions.

The following topics are covered in this chapter:

- Policies
- Events
- Conditions
- Actions
- Policy profiles
- Types of policies, that is, compliance and control
- Creating a compliance policy
- Creating a control policy
- Simulating policies

Policies

A policy in Red Hat CloudForms helps you manage the compliance and control of your hybrid cloud infrastructure. Policies are made up of events, conditions, and actions.

An event triggers a condition check, and based on the outcome of the condition, actions are executed (or not executed). Some use cases of policies would be examples such as these:

- Checking whether SELinux is in enforcing mode in all CentOS virtual machines or instances

- Shutting down a virtual machine or instance if a firewall is disabled

Events

An event is an occurrence in a hybrid cloud infrastructure that initiates the checking of a condition or set of conditions. There are eight broad functional event types available in CloudForms Management Engine, and these cannot be modified. These event types contain a set of events that can be selected, and whenever these events occur, they trigger a check of conditions.

After creating a policy, to assign events, select the desired policy, click on the **Configuration** button, and select **Edit this Policy's Event assignments**. This will load the **Event Selection** page, which will list different events categorized into sections. Some of the event categories are:

- **VM Configuration**, which contains events such as **VM Create Complete**, **VM Settings Change**, and **VM Clone Complete**.

- **VM Lifecycle**, which contains events such as **VM Discovery**, **VM Retired**, and so on.

- **VM Operation**, which contains events such as **VM Power On**, **VM Power Off**, **VM Reset**, and so on. A screenshot of the **VM Operation** section, which we will work with in our example, is shown here:

VM Operation

VDI Connecting to Session	VDI Console Login Session	VDI Disconnected from Session
VDI Login Session	VDI Logoff Session	VM Analysis Complete
VM Analysis Failure	VM Analysis Request	VM Analysis Start
VM Guest Reboot	VM Guest Reboot Request	VM Guest Shutdown
VM Guest Shutdown Request	VM Live Migration (VMOTION)	VM Power Off
VM Power Off Request	VM Power On	VM Power On Request
VM Remote Console Connected	VM Removal from Inventory	VM Removal from Inventory Request
VM Reset	VM Reset Request	VM Snapshot Create Complete
VM Snapshot Create Request	VM Snapshot Create Started	VM Standby of Guest
VM Standby of Guest Request	VM Suspend	VM Suspend Request

Conditions

Conditions are tests that are performed on the attributes of virtual machines/instances and hosts. They are categorized as either a host condition or a VM condition, and listed under the **Conditions** accordion in **Control Explorer**.

A condition consists of two important elements:

- Scope is an optional VM/instance or host attribute check
- Expression is a mandatory check

For example, we scope a condition that will apply to virtual machines (or instances) running Windows Operating Systems only, and then run an expression to check whether a specific version of an antivirus is installed.

 Note

If a policy does not have any condition, scope, or expression, then it is unconditional and always returns a `true` value.

Actions

An action is a step that is executed based on the outcome of a condition (or conditions). CloudForms Management Engine provides a set of default actions as well as an option to create custom actions. The default actions are listed as follows:

- **Cancel vCenter Task**
- **Check Host or VM Compliance**
- **Collect Running Processes on VM Guest OS**
- **Connect All CD-ROM drives for virtual machine**
- **Connect All floppy drives for virtual machine**
- **Connect All floppy and CD-ROM Drives for virtual machine**
- **Convert to template**
- **Delete all snapshots**
- **Delete most recent snapshot**
- **Delete VM from disk**
- **Disconnect All CD-ROM drives for virtual machine**
- **Disconnect All floppy drives for virtual machine**
- **Disconnect All floppy and CD-ROM Drives for virtual machine**
- **Execute an external script**

- Generate audit event
- Generate log message
- Initiate SmartState analysis for host
- Initiate SmartState analysis for VM
- Mark as non-compliant
- Prevent current event from proceeding
- Put virtual machine guest OS in standby
- Raise automation event
- Refresh data from vCenter
- Remove virtual machine from inventory
- Retire virtual machine
- Shutdown virtual machines guest OS
- Start virtual machine
- Stop virtual machine
- Suspend virtual machine

Types of policies

There are two types of policies you can create from Red Hat CloudForms Management Engine:

- A control policy
- A compliance policy

In the following topics, we will see how to create these types of policies using the examples cited earlier.

All the steps here are performed by navigating to **Control** and selecting **Explorer**.

Control policy

A control policy is used to manage the hybrid cloud environment by performing actions based on a condition's outcome. Control policies are created using events, conditions, and actions, and thus they require that we work with all of these three components.

Creating a control policy

Creating a control policy involves creating conditions, assigning events to the policy, and setting actions for the outcomes of the conditions.

To create a control policy, navigate to the **Policies** accordion in **Control Explorer**, expand **Control Policies**, and select **Vm Control Policies**. Next, click on the **Configuration** button and select **Add a New Vm Control Policy**, as shown in this screenshot:

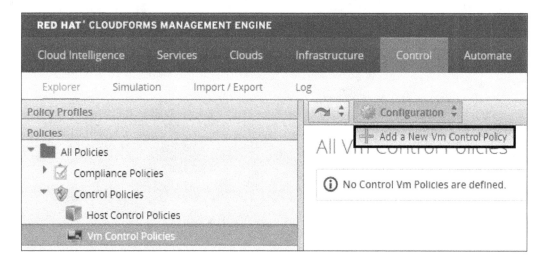

In the **Adding a new Vm Control Policy** dialog, enter a description in **Description**, ensure that the **Active** checkbox is ticked, and optionally set **Scope** and **Notes**, if required. Click on **Add** to create the Control Policy. In the following figure we are adding a new virtual machine control policy called Shutdown VM/Instance without Firewall as an example:

 Note that the **???** output highlighted in yellow will disappear on adding a scope, which can be done using the selections available below it. Since it is optional, we are not setting a scope in this example.

Creating a condition

Next, we will create a condition, and the important part of it involves creating the right expression. As an example, let's consider a condition to check whether the firewall of a VM or instance is enabled (later, our action will be to shut down the virtual machine or instance if the condition is `false`).

To create a condition, navigate to the **Conditions** accordion, expand the tree, and select **VM Conditions**. Next, click on the **Configuration** button and select **Add a new Vm Condition**. This will load the **Adding a new Condition** page.

Fill in **Description** and optionally **Scope** by clicking on the **edit pencil** icon.

> **Note**
> You will again find **???** highlighted in yellow under the **Expression** section, which will disappear after we add an expression.

Creating an expression

To create an expression, select a value from the drop-down selection area below the **Expressions** section. The following is the expression selection based on the example considered:

- **Find**
- **VM and Instance.OS.Firewall Rules : Active**
- **=**
- **true**
- **Check All**
- **Required**
- **=**
- **true**

Click on the tick mark to add the expression, as shown in the following screenshot. If two or more expressions are needed, create and add them in a similar fashion.

The final completed dialog should look something like what is shown in the following screenshot. Click on **Add** to create the condition.

Modifying or removing expressions

Following are the processes to modify or remove expressions in a control policy:

- To modify an existing expression, click on it from under **Expressions** to highlight it (in yellow), and make changes in the drop-down selection below it. Once done, click on the tick mark to save it.

- To remove an existing expression, click on it again to select it and click on the **X** mark.

Adding the condition to the control policy

To add the newly created condition to a control policy, navigate to the control policy in the **Policies** accordion, click on the **Configuration** button, and select **Edit this Policy's Condition assignments**, like this:

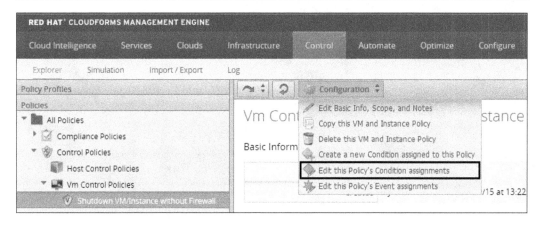

In the window that appears, select the condition from the **Available VM and Instance Conditions** list and click on the right arrow to move it to **Policy Conditions**, as shown in the following screenshot. For this example, we will select the **Firewall Enabled?** condition created earlier.

To select more than one condition, hold down the *Ctrl* key and select them. Click on **Add** when done.

Setting the events

The next step in creating a control policy is to assign the events that will trigger the condition to be tested.

To do so, click on the **Configuration** button and select **Edit this Policy's Event assignments**, as shown here:

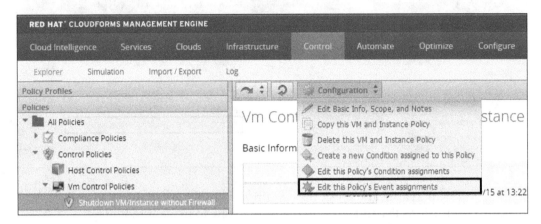

In the **Event Assignments** dialog, select the event that will trigger the condition to be tested. For this example, we will select the **VM Power On** event, as shown in the next screenshot. To select additional events, check the desired events. Click on **Save** when done.

Setting the action

The final step is to set the action (s) that will be executed based on the condition's outcome. The actions are set for situations where the condition is `true` and where it is `false`.

To set the actions, navigate to the event (for example, **VM Power On** in this case) in the **Policies** accordion. Click on the **Configuration** button and select **Edit Actions for this Policy Event**, as shown in the following screenshot:

 Note that the event can also be selected by clicking on it from the **Events** section in the control policy summary.

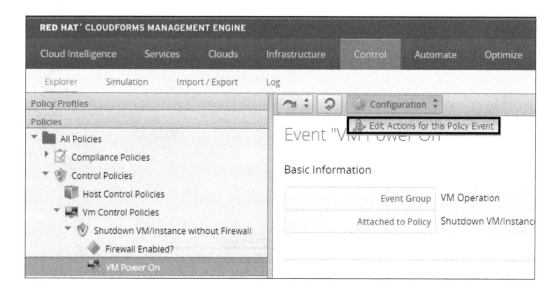

In the event edit dialog, select the actions that should be carried out for two scenarios:

- The scenario where all the conditions are `True`
- The scenario where any condition is `False`

In the example we have considered, the VM/instance should be shut down if the firewall is disabled. Hence, in this case, an action needs to be carried out when any condition is `false`. If the condition is `true`, no action is needed.

So leave **Order of Actions if ALL Conditions are True** blank and select **(S) Shutdown Virtual Machine Guest OS** for **Order of Actions if ANY conditions are False**. To select more than one action, use the *Ctrl* key, and to reorder, use the up and down arrows. Click on **Save** when done. In line to the considered example, the selection action for this control policy if any of the conditions is false is **(S)Shutdown Virtual Machine Guest OS** as shown in the following figure:

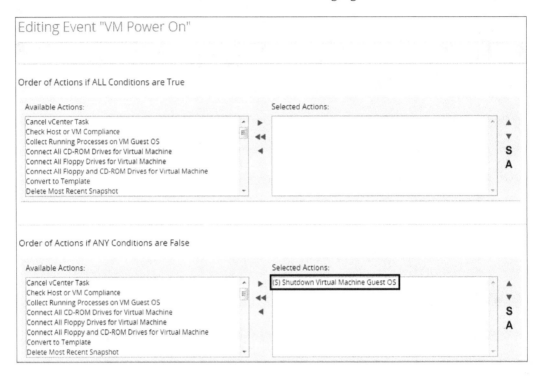

We now have a control policy in place that will shut down the VM or instances if the firewall is disabled.

Compliance policy

A compliance policy's primary purpose is to ensure the security and compliance of the hybrid cloud environment by checking certain conditions against a VM/instance or host and marking them as compliant or noncompliant. The events and actions are automatically assigned by Red Hat CloudForms Management Engine. The event is a VM compliance check or host compliance check, and the action is a result that states whether the virtual machine or instance or host is compliant or noncompliant.

Additionally, a scope expression can also be defined for a kind of pre-check when a compliance check event is triggered to only run the conditions on the items in the scope.

Creating a compliance policy

Similar to a control policy, a compliance policy is created for a VM or host. For this example, we will see how to create a VM compliance policy, and most of the steps here are similar to the working of control policies.

In **Control Explorer**, click on the **Policies** accordion on the left side, select **Compliance Policies**, and choose **Vm Compliance Policies**. Then click on the **Configuration** button and choose **Add a New Vm Compliance Policy**, as shown in the following screenshot:

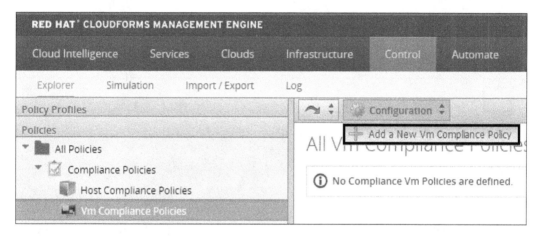

In the **Adding a new Vm Compliance Policy** dialog, provide a description under **Description**, ensure that the policy is active, optionally set a scope, and enter any notes. Click on **Add** to finish.

Creating a new condition

Conditions used in a control policy can also be used as conditions for a compliance policy. For the purpose of our example, we will go ahead and create a new condition. Let's consider an example where we want to check SELinux compliance of virtual machines or instances. If the SELinux mode is set to **enforcing**, it is compliant. Otherwise, it is noncompliant.

Follow the same steps used earlier to create a VM condition in this case. Fill in **Description** and, optionally, **Scope**.

In the **Expression** section, set the following options in the dropdowns:

- **Find**
- **VM and Instances.Files : Name**
- **=**
- **/etc/sysconfig/selinux**
- **Check Any**
- **Contents**
- **=**
- **^\s*SELINUX\s+enforcing** (this checks **SELINUX=enforcing** in the /etc/
  sysconfig/selinux file)

Click on the tick mark to add the expression to the list, and finally click on **Add** to
create the condition.

Assigning the condition to the compliance policy

Ensure that the new compliance policy is selected in the **Policies** accordion on the
left, click on the **Configuration** button, and select **Edit this Policy's Condition
assignments**, as shown here:

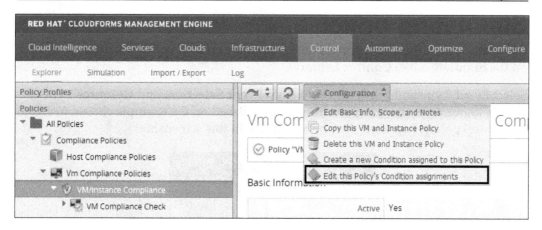

In the **Editing Vm Compliance Policy** dialog, select the required conditions for the policy from **Available VM and Instance Conditions**, and click on the right arrow to add them to the policy. When you're done, click on **Save**. In our example case, it is the **SELinux Check** condition created earlier that we use, as shown in the following screenshot:

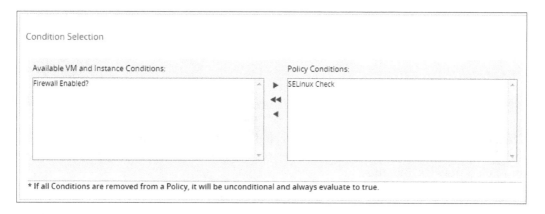

We have thus created a compliance policy that will show the status as compliant if SELinux is in enforcing mode and noncompliant otherwise. A compliance policy does not require any assignment of events or actions.

Simulating policies

Red Hat CloudForms provides options to simulate created policies. To simulate, click on the **Simulate** tab in **Control Explorer**.

Select **Event Type** and a specific event from **Event Selection**, and **Resource Type** and **Resource** from the **VM Selection** options. Based on the example chosen to create the control policy, I selected the options shown in this screenshot:

Click on **Submit** to simulate with the selected options. The results are displayed in the right pane, with the option to filter the results based on scope, passed policies, and failed policies, like this:

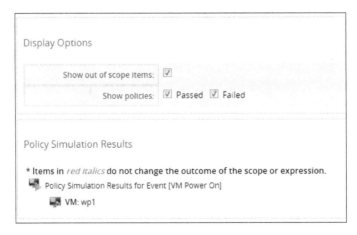

Summary

In this chapter, you learned how to manage and control a hybrid cloud infrastructure using policies. We saw how to create policies using conditions, events, and actions. We also saw how to simulate them.

In the next chapter, we will see how to monitor a hybrid cloud environment using CloudForms Management Engine.

8

Monitoring a Hybrid Cloud Infrastructure Using Red Hat CloudForms

In this chapter, you will learn about the different ways in which we can monitor and gather intelligence information about this hybrid cloud environment has to be built using CloudForms first. We will also see how to use this insight to better anticipate and take corrective actions.

The following topics are covered in this chapter:

- Dashboard
- Widgets
- Reports
- Chargeback
- Alerts
- SmartState analysis

Dashboard

The **Cloud Intelligence** dashboard, or "dashboard" as it is called, is the default view when you log in to the Red Hat CloudForms portal. This dashboard is made up of widgets that display various pieces of information about the hybrid cloud infrastructure, like this:

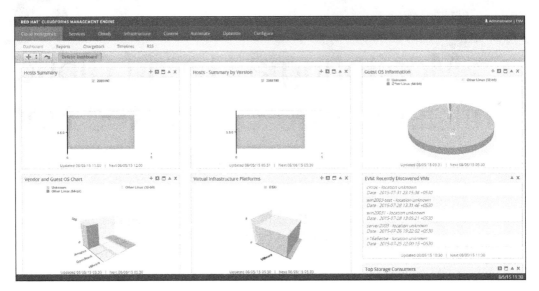

Widgets

Widgets are small apps on the dashboard that organize and display various pieces of information about the hybrid cloud infrastructure. A set of default widgets is loaded; these contain configurable items. There are nine default widgets that can be selected to display on the dashboard.

There are four different categories of widgets:

- Reports
- Charts
- RSS feeds
- Menus

Here is a screenshot that shows an example of a widget that shows **Guest OS information** in a pie chart:

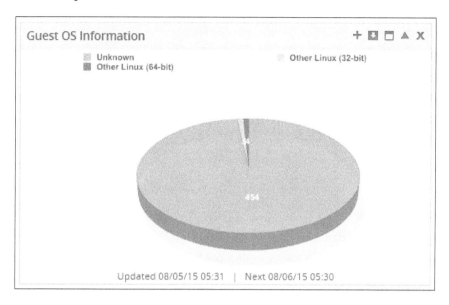

Adding a widget

To add a widget, click on the **+** button and select a widget from list, as shown in the following screenshot:

 Note
The **+** sign to add a widget may be grayed out if all the widgets are already displayed.

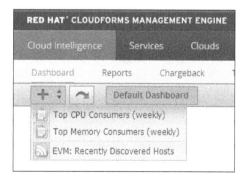

Only widgets that are not displayed are available to add.

Widget tasks from the dashboard

Once a widget is added to the dashboard, you can perform various tasks on it. To perform a task, click on the respective button in the top-right corner on the widget, as shown here:

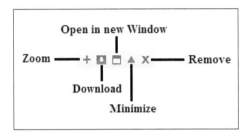

The possible tasks depend on the widget type:

- The **Charts** widget:
    - Zoom in on the chart
    - Download the chart report
    - Open the chart and the full report in a new window
    - Minimize the widget
    - Remove the widget from the dashboard

- The **Reports** widget:
    - Download the full report in PDF format
    - Open the full report in a new window
    - Minimize the widget
    - Remove the widget

- The **RSS Feeds** widget:
    - Minimize
    - Remove

- The **Menus** widget:
  - Minimize
  - Remove

Creating widgets

Red Hat CloudForms provides a way to create new widgets for the dashboard. As an example, we will look into creating a chart widget in the following steps:

1. To create a widget, select the **Reports** tab from the **Cloud Intelligence** menu. Then click on the **Dashboard Widgets** accordion and navigate to **Charts** under **All Widgets**.

2. Click on the **Configuration** button and select **Add a new Widget**, as shown in this screenshot:

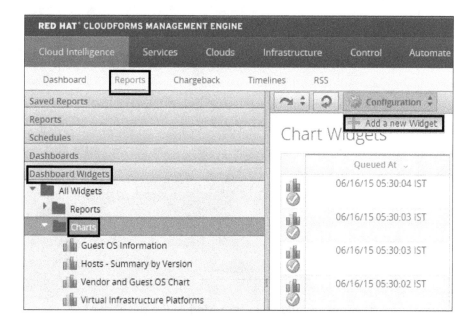

3. In the **Adding a new Widget** dialog screen, enter **Basic Information** for the widget, such as **Title** and **Description**, and make sure that it's active by checking the **Active** option.

4. Select what **Chart Report** should display by selecting **Filter** from one of the available options in the dropdown. For this example, I selected **Configuration Management/Hosts/Hosts Summary**.

5. Finally, select **Timer** (to decide how frequently it should run) and **Visibility**. The visibility can be set to **To All Users, By Role,** or **By Group**. Again, for this example, I left the defaults as they were. Click on **Add** to create the chart widget. In this example, I am adding a new widget called **Hosts Summary** with specifications as shown in the following figure:

The new chart widget is now available to be added to the dashboard.

Similar steps can be followed to create other categories of widgets, such as **Reports** widgets, **RSS Feed** widgets, or **Menus** widgets.

Additional widget operations that can be carried out are:

-   **Populating the widget content immediately**: If you do not wish to wait for the scheduled time to populate the widget content, you can schedule an immediate content generation. To do so, click on **Configuration** and select **Generate Widget content now**.

- **Editing a widget**: To edit a widget, navigate to that widget in the **Dashboard Widgets** accordion under the **Cloud Intelligence** reports, select the widget, click on **Configuration**, and select **Edit this Widget**.

- **Copying a widget**: To copy a widget, select **Copy this Widget** from the **Configuration** button.

- **Deleting a widget**: To delete a widget, select **Delete this Widget from the Database**.

The following screenshot shows the different widget operations available in a single view:

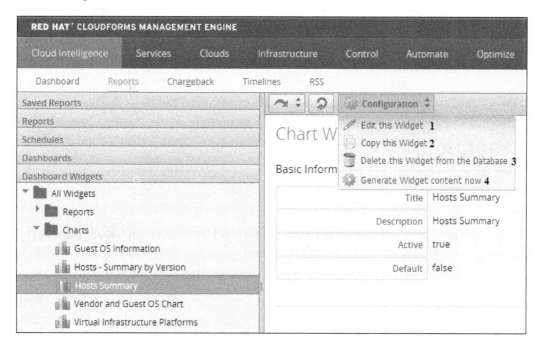

- **Import/export**: Select the **Import/Export** accordion and click on **Widgets**:

  ○ To import, click on **Browse**, point to the `.yml` extension file, and click on the **Upload** button.

  ○ To export, select **Available Widgets** (use *Ctrl* to select multiple widgets) and click on **Export**.

> **Note**
> You can only export the custom widgets created, not the default widgets.

Reports

Generating reports across the hybrid cloud infrastructure is ever easier with Red Hat CloudForms.

Cloud intelligence reports provide various insights into the hybrid cloud infrastructure about the utilization and costs. These reports can be plugged into third-party tools for further consolidation.

Red Hat CloudForms provides a default set of reports organized across different categories, folders, and subfolders. All of these cover the most common reporting patterns and data. However, you can also create custom reports.

Creating a new report

Creating a new custom report requires launching the **Adding a new report** page and filling in some information across different tabs. The new report creation page consists of nine tabs:

- **Columns**: This is where we provide basic information about the report, such as its name and what it is based on, and select the fields for it.

- **Consolidation**: This is used if there is a need to consolidate and aggregate data points to gain an insight into use cases such as performance data over a specific period of time.

- **Formatting**: This lets you set the report page size for a PDF output. You can also specify how the column headers will appear and whether any formatting needs to be applied when displaying the column values.

- **Styling**: This lets you set the text color and background displayed in a row with an option to use an `if` condition as well. This can be useful to highlight certain rows containing specific information.

- **Filter**: This lets you set parameters to filter the displayed data. You can provide a primary (record) filter, which works the same way as expressions, and a secondary (display) filter.

- **Summary**: This tab lets you set a sorting criterion if required.

- **Charts**: This lets you choose a design for the chart.

- **Timeline**: This allows you to provide a timeline setting if you wish to display events in the timeline, and provides an option for filtering.

- **Preview**: This is used to get a sneak peek into how the report looks.

Let's take an example where we want a report of all processes running inside the instances with the following fields: **Process Name**, **Process ID**, **CPU usage**, and **Memory usage**.

To begin, select **Reports** from the **Cloud Intelligence** menu item (or if you are already on the cloud intelligence dashboard, click on the **Reports** tab) and click on the **Reports** accordion. Select **All Reports**, and on the right-side, click on the **Configuration** button. Then select **Add a new Report**. This will load the **Adding a new Report** page. Let's now fill in the information required to create a report. We will visit each tab for this purpose.

The Columns tab

Fill in **Menu Name** and **Title** for the **Basic Report Info** section. In **Configure Report Columns**, select what to base the report on under **Base the report on**. The **Available Fields:** list will be populated depending on the selection in **Base the report on**. Choose the desired fields from this list by holding down the *Ctrl* key and clicking on the fields. Then press the upside-down triangle below it to add the fields to **Selected Fields:**. Finally, set the **Report Creation Timeout** value, which is optional.

For this example, I selected **Instances** for **Base the report on** and then selected five fields, as shown in the following screenshot. I am not setting a **Report Creation Timeout** value. The selected values for the **Columns** tab is as shown in the following figure:

The Consolidation tab

For this example, I have chosen not to group the records. Feel free to group them by selecting the field for up to three columns.

 Note that additional sections and fields may appear depending on selection in the columns.

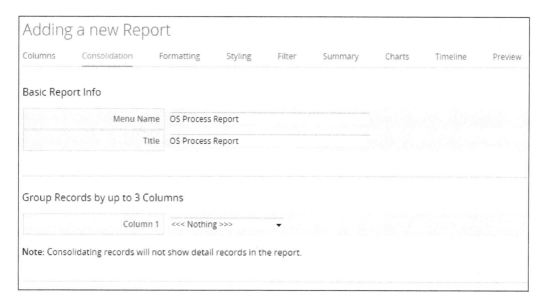

 If consolidating the report, individual records are not available.

The Formatting tab

Set a PDF output page size, column header names, and their formats under the **Specify Column Headers and Formats** section.

For this example, I have set the values shown in the following screenshot:

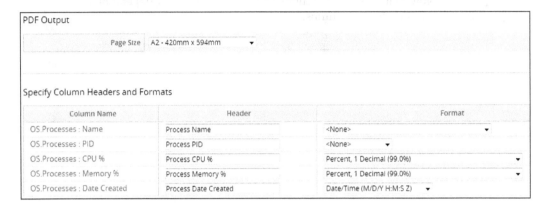

The Styling tab

For this example, I want to display a row in a red background if the process name is `httpd` and use **Gray background** for all other processes, so I set the styles like this:

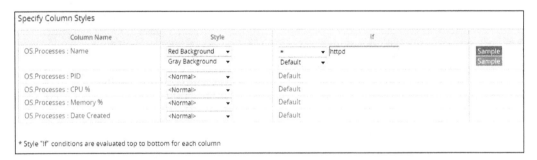

The Filter tab

For this example, I am setting **Primary (Record) Filter** and **Secondary (Display) Filter**, as shown in the following screenshot. Creating them is similar to creating expressions, which we saw in *Chapter 7, Managing Red Hat CloudForms.*

> **Note**
> To add **Secondary (Display) Filter**, click on the **Edit** button (the pencil icon).

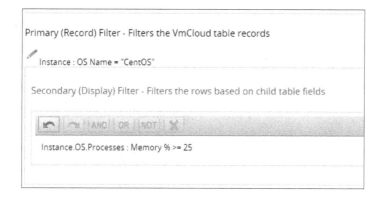

The Summary tab

Set **Sort Criteria** in the **Summary** tab. For this example, I have chosen **Sort the Report By OS.Process : Name** by setting **Ascending**, and it is without sort breaks, which is set by selecting **No** for **Show Sort Breaks**.

Additionally, I have selected to sort within the process name by memory percentage, which is set by selecting **OS.Process : Memory** % for the **Within Above Field, Sort By** field. Feel free to play around for the desired results.

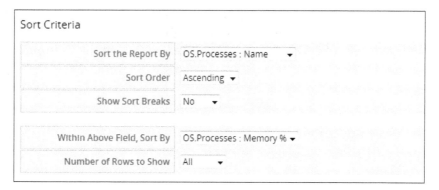

The Charts tab

In the **Charts** tab, select a design that also shows a sample of what the chart will look like. I selected the values shown in this screenshot:

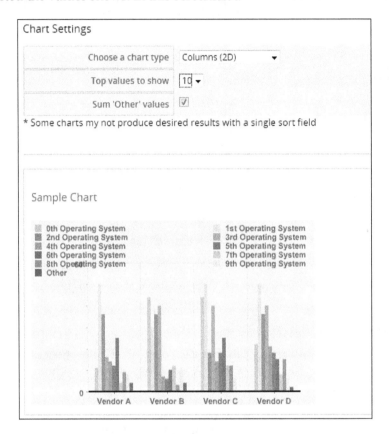

The Timeline tab

The **Timeline** tab works only if a time-related field has been selected in the fields to display. If not, it takes you back to the **Columns** tab to add a time-related field. In this example, let's select the **OS.Process : Date Created** field in the **Columns** tab.

Set the **Timeline Settings** fields as desired, as shown in the following screenshot. This also shows a sample for a visual feel.

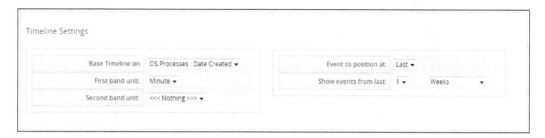

The Preview tab

The **Preview** tab shows a preview of the chart, timeline, and report views. Initially, this tab is blank, and a preview is generated only after you've clicked on the **Load** button.

Click on **Add** when done.

 Note that it is possible that the preview shows no statistics or data for the chart, timeline, or report, as there may not be enough information for fresh setups.

Running a report

You can run a report either manually or on schedule. Once a request to generate a report is placed, it is queued, and a visual status indicator shows when the report is completed and ready for viewing or downloading:

- To run a report manually, click on the **Reports** accordion and select the desired report. Then click on the **Queue** button. This loads the **Saved Reports** tab for that report, with the status appearing as **Queued**. To refresh the status, click on the **Reload current display** button. Once the status shows *finished* (a green check mark), click on the report to view it.

- To schedule a report, select the **Report**, click on the **Configuration** button, and select **Add a new Schedule**. In the dialog that appears, fill in **Basic Information**, such as **Name** and **Description**, and ensure that the schedule is active. Next, provide the schedule details, such as how frequently to run (once, hourly, daily, weekly, or monthly), the time zone, the starting date, and the starting time. You can also choose to e-mail the report with attachments in a **Text**, **CSV** or **PDF** format. When done, click on **Add**. This adds the schedule to the **Schedules** accordion in the **Reports** tab in **Cloud Intelligence**.

  ° You can now modify this schedule from the **Schedules** accordion by clicking on the **Configuration** button and selecting **Edit this Schedule**.

  ° You can also run the schedule immediately by clicking on the **Configuration** button and selecting **Queue up this Schedule to run now**.

Viewing and downloading reports

Once reports are generated, they are automatically added to **Saved Reports** for future viewing. **Saved Reports** can be viewed in different ways:

- By clicking on **Report Instance** under the **Saved Reports** tab of the report in the **Reports** accordion
- Directly from the **Saved Reports** accordion by selecting **Report Instance**

Some reports support multiple viewing options, such as graphs, tabular or lists. This depends on what type of data the report handles and how they were created. Reports can also be downloaded (after generation) in formats such as text, CSV, and PDF.

For example, I have a saved report here for **VMs Not Power On**. Clicking on the **Download** button (the down arrow icon) to the extreme right will show a dropdown to select one of the report formats. Clicking on a format (PDF in this case), as shown in the following screenshot, will send a request to generate a report and prompt with a download dialog when ready:

Here is an example of a downloaded PDF report:

Other report operations

Now that you know how reports can be created, run, and viewed or downloaded, there a few other report operations that you should be aware of:

- Reports can easily be copied, thus enabling us to create new reports quickly by changing only a few parameters. To do so select **Report**, click on the **Configuration** button, and select **Copy this report**. Then make the required changes and click on **Add**.

- To make any changes to the report, simply select **Edit this Report** from the **Configuration** button.

- To delete the report, select **Delete this Report from the Database**.

Importing/exporting reports

Click on the **Import/Export** accordion under the **Reports** tab in **Cloud Intelligence** and select **Custom Reports**:

- To import, click on **Browse**, point to the location of the `.yml` file, click on **Ok**, and then click on **Upload**

- To export, select the report from the list of available reports and click on **Export**

Usage

The **Usage** option in **Cloud Intelligence** dashboard provides a way to collect resource usage metrics, such as the CPU, RAM, disk space, disk I/O, and network I/O. There are two prerequisites, however, for being able to collect usage information:

- The virtual machines for which the usage information needs to be collected must be tagged

- Capacity and utilization collection must be enabled

To start viewing the usage data, select **Cloud Intelligence** and then select **Usage**. In the dialog box that appears, select a date for which to show the usage data under **Date**, the period (either **Day** or **Hour**) under **Period**, the tag category, and finally the tag entry itself.

Chargeback

The **Chargeback** feature in Red Hat CloudForms Management Engine helps you create a pricing structure and bill for virtual machine usage. The billing is either based on the ownership tag or the company tag.

There is a prerequisite for chargeback:

Chargeback requires that Capacity & Utilization data collection must be enabled in the **Server Control** settings. To do this, click on the **Configure** menu option and select **Configuration**. This will load the server settings page. Under the **Server Control** section, **Capacity & Utilization Coordinator**, **Capacity & Utilization Data Collector**, and **Capacity & Utilization Data Processor** must be checked, as shown here:

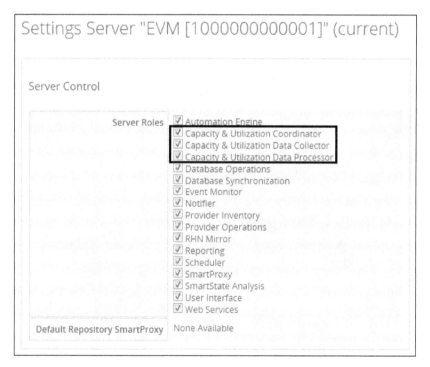

Chargeback in CloudForms comes with two default rates, one each for **Compute and Storage**, but you can also create custom rates:

- Creating compute rates helps you set the costs for CPU, disk I/O, memory, network I/O, and fixed items
- Creating storage rates help you charge for fixed and storage items

Working with rates involves three steps:

1. Create **Chargeback Rates** (or use default ones).
2. Assign **Chargeback Rates** to the desired infrastructure resource.
3. Create a **Chargeback Report**.

Creating a Chargeback rate

To create a **Chargeback Rate**, navigate to **Cloud Intelligence** and then to **Chargeback**. Select the **Rates** accordion and choose **Compute** or **Storage**. Click on the **Configuration** button and select **Add a new Chargeback Rate**. In the dialog box that appears, enter the rate for the resource item that you wish to charge for and the **Per Time** value (which can be hourly, daily, weekly, or monthly). Click on **Add** when done.

For this book, we will use the default rate available.

Assigning a Chargeback rate

Once we have a chargeback rate, we need to assign it to a corresponding infrastructure resource:

- Compute chargeback rates are assigned to one of the following resource types: the enterprise, the selected **Clusters**, the selected **Infrastructure Providers**, or **Tagged VMs and Instances**
- Storage chargeback rates are assigned to one of the following: the **Enterprise**, selected **Datastores**, or **Tagged Datastores**

To assign a chargeback rate, click on the **Assignments** accordion under **Chargeback**, which is under **Cloud Intelligence**, and select either **Compute** or **Storage**. From the right pane, select the **Assign To** value and then select the chargeback rate you wish to assign to the items. You can assign different chargeback rates to different items, for example, a different rate for instances running on EC2 and a different rate for instances running on OpenStack. Click on **Save** when done.

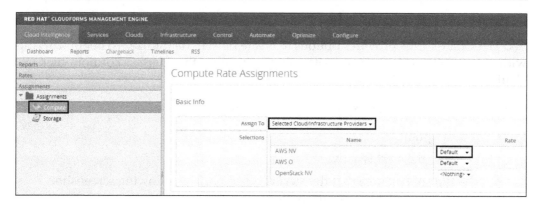

Creating a Chargeback report

Finally, you can also create a chargeback report for monitoring. To create a chargeback report, follow the usual steps for creating a report and set the **Base the report on** parameter to **Chargebacks** from the dropdown in the **Columns** tab.

Alerts

Alerts are a way of notifying changes and threshold limits in a hybrid cloud environment. This is done through either an e-mail or an SNMP trap. Before we can work with creating and using alerts, a couple of prerequisites need to be performed:

- Enable the **Notifier** server role by the following steps:
    1. Navigate to **Configure** and then to **Configuration**.
    2. On the server settings page, under the **Server Control** section, select the **Notifier** role and then click on **Save**.

- Configure the SNMP and SMTP

Alerts can be created for virtual machines, instances, and CloudForms Management Engine operations.

They can be created for each of these categories based on some default values provided by CloudForms Management Engine, or using custom expressions.

Creating a new alert

Red Hat CloudForms provides options to create new alerts for use. To begin working with alerts, click on **Control** and select **Explorer**. Select the **Alerts** accordion, click on **Configuration**, and select **Add a new Alert**.

Creating a new alert involves providing the following information:

- A description.
- Whether the alert is active.
- The type of resource that the alert is based on. The following screenshot shows the available resource options:

- What to evaluate. The options displayed here change depending on what is selected in **Based On**. This screenshot depicts them:

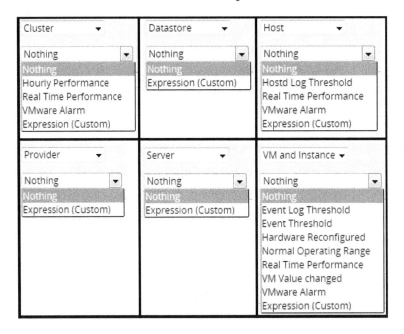

Note that if the **What to Evaluate** option is set to **Nothing** or **Expression (Custom)**, a **Driving Event** field with a dropdown appears, where we can select from a list of events. Additionally, the **Expression (Custom)** option requires an expression to be created in a way similar to what we did when creating conditions.

- The notification frequency, which varies from once a minute to once a day.

- The parameters section displays specific parameters depending on the value selected in **What to Evaluate**. For example, if **Event Threshold** is selected, the **Event Threshold** parameters, such as what **Event to Check**, **How Far Back to Check**, and **Event Count Threshold**, need to be provided.

- The e-mail, here, we choose whom to notify about the alert, by either selecting a user from the list (RHCFME users) or by entering an e-mail address manually.

To enter an e-mail address manually, type it in the field and click on the green + button.

- Check **SNMP Trap** if you wish to trap the alert. This will require you to provide an IP address of the machine to send the trap to, choose the version, and — depending on the version — either enter a trap number (for v1) or a trap object ID (for v2).

- Choosing whether to display this event on the timeline.

- Also, we have to choose whether to send a management event for an automation process. Sending a management event notification is done by checking the check box and requires you to provide an event name under **Event Name**.

Creating an alert example

As an example, we will see how to create a virtual machine and instance alert to notify us if there is a **VM/Instance Power Off** event.

In **Control Explorer**, click on the **Alerts** accordion, then click on the **Configuration** button, and select **Add a new Alert**.

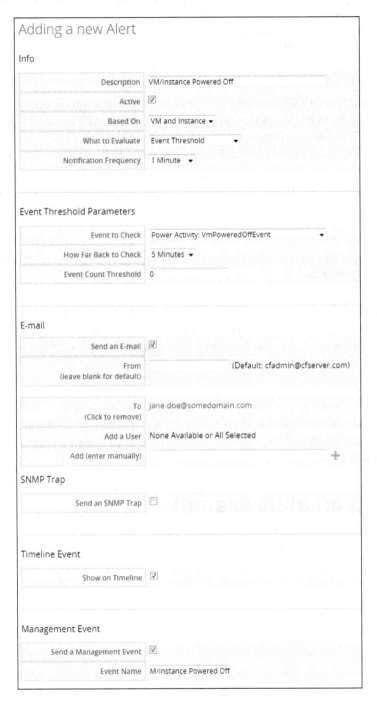

Other alert operations

Alerts can also be edited, copied or deleted. Let's take a look at how this is done in the following points:

- To edit an alert, select the alert from the **Alert** accordion in **Control Explorer**, click on **Configuration**, and select **Edit this Alert**

- To copy an alert, select **Copy this Alert** from the **Configuration** button and click on **OK** to confirm

- To delete an alert, select the **Delete this Alert** option from the **Configuration** button and confirm by clicking on **OK**

SmartState analysis

SmartState analysis is a key feature of Red Hat CloudForms Management Engine. It uses SmartProxy to extract internal information of a virtual machine—such as user accounts, applications, software patches, and so on—and processes all of this. Every zone must have at least one CloudForms management server with the SmartState role enabled.

There are more prerequisites for this:

- SmartState Analysis role has to be enabled in the **Server Control** Settings
- SmartProxy has to be enabled in the **Server Control** Settings
- SmartProxy has to be installed on the host running the virtual machines with visibility to the data store (the storage location)

There are other infrastructure\vendor-specific requirements, and you should refer to them before running a SmartState analysis on them.

SmartProxy

SmartProxy is a program within the Red Hat CloudForms Management engine that, when enabled on the Management Engine server (or installed on a remote host), analyzes the virtual machines registered or running on the host. It can also analyze templates associated with a provider.

Running a SmartState analysis

To manually run a SmartState analysis on a single virtual machine template or a set of virtual machines or templates, click on **Infrastructure** and then select **Virtual Machines**. Choose the desired virtual machines and templates to analyze, click on the **Configuration** button, and select **Perform SmartState Analysis**, as shown in the following screenshot:

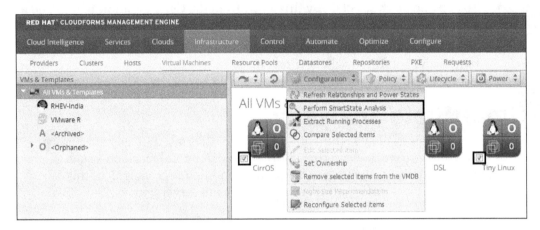

Click on **OK** to confirm. If successful, a message is displayed with a green check stating that the **SmartState Analysis** has been initiated.

To view the results, click on any one of the VMs for which the Smart State analysis was performed to load the details page. Sections such as **Security** and **Configuration** will show the VM or instance's internal details, such as the number of **Users**, **Packages**, **Init Processes**, and so on.

Summary

In this chapter, you learned how to monitor the hybrid cloud infrastructure in different ways, such as using widgets in the **Cloud Intelligence** dashboard, by generating reports, and by creating alerts. We also saw how to use chargeback for billing of resources and how to generate reports based on chargeback. Finally, you learned about the SmartState analysis, which helps gather information that is internal for a virtual machine.

In the next chapter, we will cover how to view and use trends in the hybrid setup to perform capacity planning and optimization.

9
Optimizing Using Red Hat CloudForms

In this chapter, you will learn about the different features available with Red Hat CloudForms to aid us in optimizing the hybrid cloud infrastructure.

The following topics are covered in this chapter:

- Optimization
- Collecting capacity and utilization data
- Charts
- Utilization
- Planning
- Bottlenecks

Optimization

Optimization in Red Hat CloudForms includes tasks such as viewing the utilization trends across a region, data store and so on. You can plan where to move or create new virtual machines and check the areas of bottlenecks in your virtual infrastructure based on capacity, utilization, or both in the form of a report or on the timeline.

Collecting capacity and utilization data

For us to be able to perform optimization tasks, capacity and utilization data must be collected from across the virtual infrastructure in the hybrid cloud environment. Red Hat CloudForms provides certain server roles that, when enabled, collect this data, which can then be used to see trends and perform capacity planning for the future. There are three server roles that facilitate the collection and processing of capacity and utilization metrics. They are as follows:

- **Capacity and utilization coordinator**: This role basically acts as a scheduler and, at the correct time, queues a capacity and utilization collection job. In a single zone, there can only be one such role active at a time.

- **Capacity and utilization data collector**: This role actions or performs the job that is queued by the capacity and utilization coordinator. There can be more than one CFME servers running this role and functioning at the same time.

- **Capacity and utilization data processor**: This role processes the data so that CloudForms can create charts from it. Two or more CFME servers can have this role enabled and functioning at the same time.

Enabling data collection

To enable data collection the aforementioned server roles must be enabled on the Red Hat CloudForms Management Engine server. This can be done by going to **Configure | Configuration** and checking the roles in the **Server Control** section.

In addition to this, if data needs to be collected for clusters and data stores as well, we must specify them.

Prerequisites for capacity and utilization data collection

Different virtual infrastructures (in some cases, separate versions of a particular virtual infrastructure as well) have different prerequisites steps that need to be performed before capacity and utilization data can be collected.

Note
Prior knowledge or experience of working on the respective platforms is required to perform the prerequisites.

Red Hat Enterprise virtualization

The following is an overview of the steps required to be performed in the Red Hat Enterprise Virtualization Management server to enable data collection:

1. Create a new CloudForms Management Engine user with superuser rights in the RHEV-M database, which is usually a PostgreSQL database installed on the RHEV-M server itself.

2. Update the firewall on the RHEV-M server to accept requests on port 5432.

3. Modify the pg_hba.conf file on the server to enable external MD5 authentication.

4. Also update the postgresql.conf file to allow listening for remote connections.

5. Reload the PostgreSQL configuration. This can be done from the bash shell using the service postgresql reload command or the SQL command: SELECT pg_reload_conf();

6. Add this new user to the **Provider** configuration in CFME. To do so, navigate to **Infrastructure** and then to **Providers**. Select the **Provider** option, click on the **Configuration** button, and select **Edit this Provider**. Under **Credentials**, click on **Capacity & Utilization Database** and enter the new user credentials. Click on **Save** when done.

7. Restart the **Capacity & Utilization Data Collector** role.

The Red Hat Enterprise Linux OpenStack platform

1. Install the ceilometer service (if it is not already installed).

 Note

If the installation fails, ensure that the required Red Hat channels are added and updated.

2. Install MongoDB and ensure that it is running.

3. Create a user in Ceilometer for CFME (with admin privileges).

4. Configure the keystone auth token and update the new user details in the ceilometer.conf file.

5. Start (restart) the Ceilometer service.

6. Create an endpoint for the Ceilometer service in keystone.

7. Modify the firewall to allow access to Ceilometer from outside.

For more information on the Ceilometer service and details on installing and using it, you can refer to a very good read at https://www.rdoproject.org/CeilometerQuickStart.

Data collection

Data is collected for the following infrastructure resource types: hosts, clusters, virtual machines, and data stores. This data is eventually available in the capacity and utilization charts. The following table shows what data is collected for these resources:

	CPU usage	CPU states	Disk I/O	Memory usage	Network I/O	Running VMs	Running hosts
Cluster	√	√	√	√	√	√	√
Host	√	√	√	√	√	√	×
Virtual machine	√	√	√	√	√	×	×

Similarly, the Capacity & Utilization role also collects data for datastores on space by VM type, virtual machines, and hosts.

- The Space by VM Type collects the following information:
    - Used disk space
    - Disk file space
    - Snapshot file space
    - Memory file space
    - NonVM file space
- The following information is gathered for virtual machines and hosts:
    - Number of VMs by type
    - Hosts
    - Virtual machines using datastores

Charts

Charts provide a graphical view of capacity consumption and utilization across the virtual infrastructure. Depending on what data is collected, the information is grouped for average, maximum or minimum of the values, and trends.

 Note that at least full 24-hour data is required for displaying the capacity and utilization charts.

Viewing capacity and utilization charts

Capacity and utilization charts can be viewed for a host, a cluster, or a specific virtual machine. Let's see an example in which we want to view utilization charts for a virtual machine, and see the steps involved:

1. Click on the **Infrastructure** menu item and select **Virtual Machines**.

2. Under the **VMs & Templates** accordion, click on **All VMs & Templates** and then click on the desired virtual machine, as shown in the following screenshot. You can also navigate directly to the desired virtual machine from the **VMs & Templates** accordion.

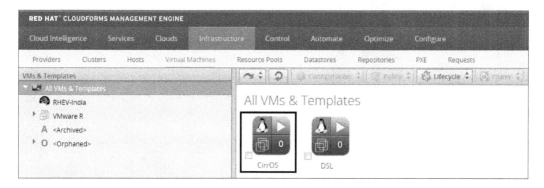

3. This will load a summary page for the virtual machine. Click on the **Monitoring** button and select **Utilization**, like this:

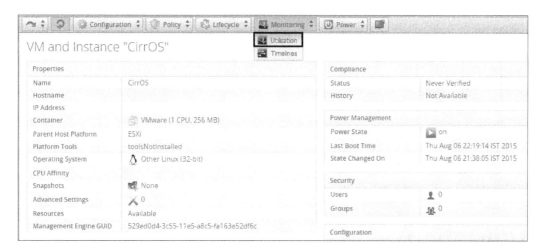

This will load the capacity and utilization data page for that specific virtual machine, as shown here:

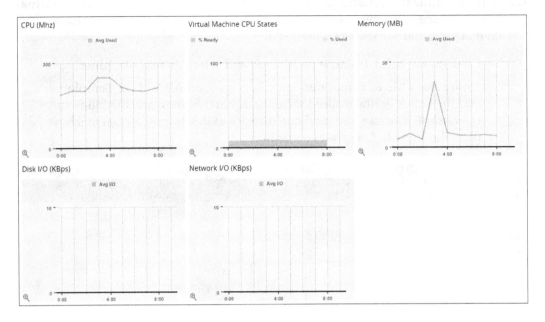

The preceding chart is from an hourly interval and currently does not have statistics for disk I/O and network I/O, as they have been recently added. In the **Options** section above this chart, you can change parameters such as the **Interval**, **Date**, and **Compare To** values to modify the chart as per your needs.

Note that if you have just added the provider, created a virtual machine, or enabled the C&U roles, no data may be available. The soonest you can view some data is after 10 minutes. This also requires changing **Interval** to **Hourly**. Daily interval data is available only for a full 24-hour day.

The steps for viewing charts for a host or cluster are quite similar. Instead of selecting a virtual machine, we select **Hosts** or **Clusters** from the **Infrastructure** menu item and then click on the desired host or cluster.

Utilization

This feature provides a utilization trend summary and reports of resources across providers and data stores.

Viewing utilization trends

You can view an overall summary, dive into details, and view reports of the utilization trends collected. To view the **Utilization** trends, click on **Optimize** and select **Utilization**. Choose the desired **Cluster**, **Provider**, or **Datastore** resource from the left and click on a tab on the right to view them in a particular way.

For example, in the following screenshot, I have shown a cluster utilization trend summary. To load this, I navigated to a cluster called **India** under a VMware environment in the **Utilization** accordion. The utilization summary is loaded by default.

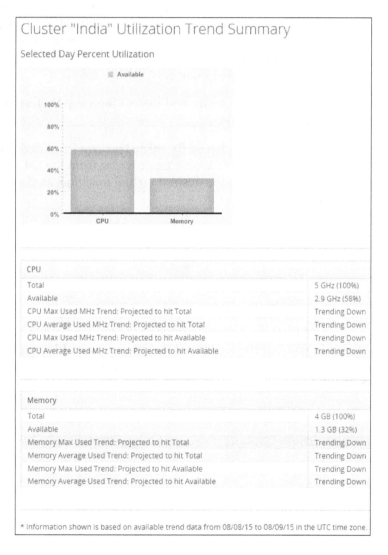

Additional options for changes to the data being displayed are also available when viewing utilization trends. You can choose **Trends for past** to calculate trends for a duration in the past, **Classification** to filter based on tags, **Time Profile**, and **Time Zone**.

Apart from summaries, you can also view additional details about the resource from the **Details** tab, and generate a report from the **Report** tab.

Planning for new virtual machines

The planning feature of Red Hat CloudForms helps decide where to provision new virtual machines using the data collected for capacity and utilization. This process involves using an existing virtual machine as a reference, selecting a source type to project the requirements, and targeting it against hosts or clusters. Let's look at the steps involved in planning in a detailed manner.

To begin with, click on the **Optimize** menu and select **Planning**. Perform the following selections from the left pane:

1. In **Reference VM Selection**, choose **By Infrastructure Provider**. This will display an additional dropdown. Select a provider from the list and then, in the third dropdown, select the desired virtual machine, as shown in this screenshot:

    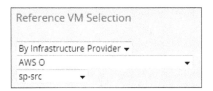

2. Next, under **VM Options**, select a source in the **Source** field to base your projections on. You can choose from **Allocation**, **Manual Input**, **Reservation**, and **Usage**. For this example, I selected **Allocation** and left the other values at default, as shown here:

    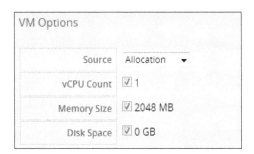

3. In the **Target Options / Limits** section, select whether to target the virtual machine against **Clusters** or **Hosts** (requires to select the **Host** category) and choose **vCPUs per Core**, **Memory Size** and **Datastore Space** based on the sizing of your virtual infrastructure. For this example, I selected **All Hosts** and left the rest at their default values, as follows:

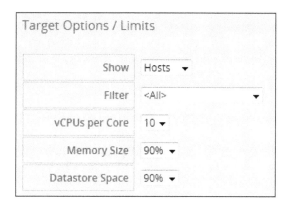

4. Finally, set **Trend Options** such as duration of the trend to base on which is set in **Trends for past** field and the **Time Profile** parameter.

5. Click **Submit**.

This generates the planning summary and report. The **Summary** tab, which provides information on the best clusters or hosts to provision your virtual machine on, and the **Report** tab can be used with the information in a more detailed format along with an option to download a PDF file of the report.

Bottlenecks

CloudForms' optimization features also include a provision to view bottlenecks across your virtual infrastructure in the form of a summary or a report. To view bottlenecks, select **Bottleneck** from the **Optimize** menu. Choose the desired resource level on the left, such as **Clusters**, **Providers**, and **Datastores**. Choose the appropriate tab, that is, **Summary** or **Report**, based on the requirement. Then select the parameters for a range of options that define how the data is to be displayed.

The options include choosing the following:

- Event groups: this option lets you choose whether to display both capacity & utilization data or only one of them.
- Whether or not to show the host events, this is set by either checking or clearing the check box.
- Setting the time zone

When viewing the **Bottleneck** information in **Summary**, you can click on a specific bottleneck to see more information.

Summary

In this chapter, you learned different ways to optimize the hybrid cloud infrastructure, such as viewing **Capacity & Utilization trends** and **Bottlenecks** and performing planning on where to provision new resources.

In the next chapter, we will peep into the supported APIs for integration requirements. It will simply be a know-how rather than deep dive into how to use them.

10

APIs for Red Hat CloudForms

Application Programming Interfaces (**APIs**) are sets of specifications and programming instructions that allow other programs and pieces of software to communicate with Red Hat CloudForms. In this chapter, you will learn about the supported APIs for Red Hat CloudForms, and we will specifically look into working with REST APIs, which are very common.

The following topics will be covered in this chapter:

- Supported APIs
- REST APIs
- Accessing Red Hat CloudForms abstractions using REST APIs
- Examples of REST API access
- SOAP APIs

Supported APIs

Red Hat CloudForms provides APIs to integrate external systems and initiate provisioning and other tasks through Red Hat CloudForms. CloudForms provides support for two types of APIs for this purpose:

- REST APIs
- SOAP APIs

REST API

Representational State Transfer (**REST**) is an APIs that works with standard HTTP and HTTPS protocols as a URL.

Accessing REST APIs

In CloudForms, REST can be accessed by prefixing the URL with /api, as follows:

`https://<FQDN>/api`

Here, FQDN is the public and fully-qualified domain name of the CloudForms server. Writing /api/ causes the current API version to be used by default, but you can also mention the version in the URL to target a specific version, for example, /api/V0.5.

When accessing it locally from the server, use the URL as follows:

`http://localhost:3000/api`

Port 3000 is the default port.

Content types

The Red Hat CloudForms API uses **JavaScript Object Notation (JSON)** format. JSON, based on the JavaScript programming language, is basically a format for data exchange and storing. One of the important advantages of JSON is its ease of use, both for humans and machines.

The content type is application/JSON for all API requests and responses.

An example of a CloudForms virtual machine provision request in JSON format is as follows:

```
{
  "version" : "1.1",
  "template_fields" : {
    "guid" : "529ed0d4-3c55-11e5-a8c5-fa163e52df6c"
  },
  "vm_fields" : {
    "number_of_sockets" : 1,
    "cores_per_socket" : 2,
    "vm_name" : "iis-webserver-2012",
    "vm_memory" : "4096",
    "vlan" : "nic1"
  },
  "requester" : {
    "user_name" : "johndoe",
    "owner_first_name" : "John",
    "owner_last_name" : "Doe",
    "owner_email" : "johndoe@somedomain.com",
    "auto_approve" : true
```

```
  },
  "tags" : {
    "network_location" : "Internal",
    "cc" : "001"
  },
  "additional_values" : {
    "request_id" : "5010"
  },
  "ems_custom_attributes" : { },
  "miq_custom_attributes" : { }
}
```

This is used along with the POST method of the REST API:

```
POST /api/provision_requests
```

Supported HTTP methods for REST API

The following is a table showing supported HTTP methods that are used along with the preceding URL formats:

Method	Description
GET	Return a specific resource (or all resources) of a collection
POST	This can be used to create a resource in the collection or perform an action on a resource
PUT	Update a resource
PATCH	Update a resource
DELETE	Delete a resource

For example the REST API command, POST /api/vms/1 is used to perform an action on a Resource (in this case the specific virtual machine identified by id 1) on a virtual machine collection.

Accessing collections, resources, and subcollections

Red Hat CloudForms provides the following URL format for access to collections, resources, and subcollections through REST APIs.

Collections

The /api/:collection URL path format represents accessing of collections such as services, virtual machines, and hosts. Let's take a look at the different collection queries that are currently possible with REST API and their respective URLs:

- **Services**: /api/services
- **Service Templates**: /api/service_templates
- **Service Catalogs**: /api/service_catalogs
- **Clusters**: /api/clusters
- **Datastores**: /api/data_stores
- **Hosts**: /api/hosts
- **Providers**: /api/providers
- **Resource Pools**: /api/resource_pools
- **EVM Servers**: /api/servers
- **Templates**: /api/templates
- **Vms**: /api/vms
- **Zones**: /api/zones
- **Policies**: /api/policies
- **Policy Profiles**: /api/policy_profiles
- **Groups**: /api/groups
- **Roles**: /api/roles
- **Users**: /api/users
- **Requests**: /api/requests
- **Service Requests**: /api/service_requests
- **Request Tasks**: /api/request_tasks
- **Automation Requests**: /api/automation_requests
- **Provision Requests**: /api/provision_requests

Let's consider an example where we want to list all hosts (hosts being the collection here) in the CloudForms environment. I am running this command on the CloudForms Management Engine server.

Note

Make sure that cURL is installed on the machine from which you are running the command. To install cURL, run `yum install curl`/`apt-get install curl`.

The `curl` command is as follows:

```
# curl --user admin:smartvm -i -X GET -H "Accept: application/json"
http://localhost:3000/api/hosts
```

The output will be similar to something like this:

```
{"name":"hosts","count":4,"subcount":4,"resources":[{"href":"http://localhost:3000/api
/hosts/1000000000004"},{"href":"http://localhost:3000/api/hosts/1000000000003"},{"href
":"http://localhost:3000/api/hosts/1000000000001"},{"href":"http://localhost:3000/api/
hosts/1000000000002"}]}
```

Resources

The URL format for accessing a specific resource in the collection is `/api/:collection/:id`. Let's consider an example where we want to get information about a specific virtual machine in a virtual machine collection.

Run the following command for the same, where `1000000074058` is the ID of the virtual machine for this example:

Note

The virtual machine ID for your setup could be different, and so the ID of the virtual machine is required, which can be obtained by running a `curl` command for the list of virtual machines. The URL format for this will be `http://localhost:3000/api/vms/`, similar to the one we ran to list all hosts.

```
# curl --user admin:smartvm -i -X GET -H "Accept: application/json"
http://localhost:3000/api/vms/1000000074058
```

This will produce an output similar to the following screenshot:

```
{"id":"http://localhost:3000/api/vms/1000000074058","vendor":"vmware","name":"CirrOS","locatio
n":"CirrOS/CirrOS.vmx","host_id":1000000000002,"created_on":"2015-08-06T16:08:06Z","updated_on
":"2015-08-07T15:57:42Z","storage_id":1000000000004,"guid":"529ed0d4-3c55-11e5-a8c5-fa163e52df
6c","ems_id":1000000000014,"last_scan_attempt_on":"2015-08-06T16:15:55Z","uid_ems":"564d24e5-4
9e4-12b7-ab4f-b09edec3f1ef","boot_time":"2015-08-07T03:48:03Z","tools_status":"toolsNotInstall
ed","standby_action":"powerOnSuspend","power_state":"on","state_changed_on":"2015-08-06T16:08:
05Z","connection_state":"connected","last_perf_capture_on":"2015-08-07T15:57:00Z","memory_rese
rve":0,"memory_reserve_expand":false,"memory_limit":-1,"memory_shares":2560,"memory_shares_lev
el":"normal","cpu_reserve":0,"cpu_reserve_expand":false,"cpu_limit":-1,"cpu_shares":1000,"cpu_
shares_level":"normal","template":false,"ems_ref_obj":"--- !ruby/string:VimString\nstr: vm-47\
nxsiType: :ManagedObjectReference\nvimType: :VirtualMachine\n","vdi":false,"linked_clone":fals
e,"fault_tolerance":false,"type":"VmVmware","ems_ref":"vm-47","cloud":false,"raw_power_state":
"poweredOn"}
```

Subcollections

The URL format for accessing a subcollection in the resource is /api/:collection/
:id/:subcollection. The following are the supported subcollections at the time of
writing this book:

- **Service templates**: /api/collection/id/service_templates
- **Tags**: /api/collection/id/tags
- **Automation request tasks**: /api/automation_requests/id/request_
  tasks or /api/automation_requests/id/tasks (alias of request_tasks)
- **Provision request tasks**: /api/provision_requests/id/request_tasks or
  /api/provision_requests/id/tasks (alias of request_tasks)

Let's look at another example showcasing how to use an API to retrieve information
about a subcollection, in this case tags.

The curl command for this purpose is as follows:

```
# curl --user admin:smartvm -i -X GET -H "Accept: application/json"
http://localhost:3000/api/vms/1000000074058/tags
```

The output will be something similar to this:

```
{"name":"tags","count":138,"subcount":1,"resources":[{"href":"http://localhost:3000/ap
i/vms/1000000074058/tags/1000000000138"}],"actions":[{"name":"assign","method":"post",
"href":"http://localhost:3000/api/vms/1000000074058/tags"},{"name":"unassign","method"
:"post","href":"http://localhost:3000/api/vms/1000000074058/tags"}]}
```

Further reading on REST APIs for Red Hat CloudForms

For more in-depth and detailed information on how to use REST APIs, visit https://access.redhat.com/documentation/en-US/Red_Hat_CloudForms/3.1/html/Management_Engine_5.3_Integration_Services_Guide/part-REST_API.html.

SOAP APIs

Red Hat CloudForms also supports SOAP APIs, but this will eventually be phased out. There is a collection of web services available that are categorized under **Insight**, **Control** and **Automate**:

- **Insight** web services are related to data collected by virtual infrastructure
- **Control** web services are related to policies and governance
- **Automate** web services are related to creation of workflows and provisioning of resources

Calling a Web Services Description Language (WSDL)

You can call WSDL using many web service clients, such as Windows PowerShell. Scripts, syntax, and formats vary from one client to another.

Further reading on SOAP APIs for Red Hat CloudForms

For a list of web services available under each of these categories and the WSDL library, visit https://access.redhat.com/documentation/en-US/Red_Hat_CloudForms/3.1/html/Management_Engine_5.3_Integration_Services_Guide/part-SOAP_API.html.

Summary

In this chapter, we learned about the supported APIs and how to use REST APIs to request and read Red Hat CloudForms resources so that they can be used to integrate third-party systems with Red Hat CloudForms.

Red Hat CloudForms is a huge feature-packed hybrid cloud management platform that supports a variety of cloud and virtual infrastructures, with support for more in progress, and contains a variety of features aimed at different management levels. This gives an opportunity to further our knowledge on this platform by trying to add more providers, such as Red Hat Enterprise Virtualization and the Microsoft Hyper-V based System Center Virtual Machine Manager. Working with different automation scenarios and finding out how Red Hat CloudForms can simplify the management of infrastructures, experimenting with different types of alerts, charts, and reports for monitoring and tracking are some of the areas one can explore deeper to maximize productivity and have better control over the cloud and virtual infrastructures.

Index

A

action 87
adaptive management platform 6
alerts
  about 123
  creating 124, 125
  example, creating 125
  operations 127
Amazon EC2
  adding, as cloud provider 26, 27
Amazon EC2 instance, provisioning
  about 43, 44
  Catalog tab 47
  Customize tab 49
  Environment tab 47
  Properties tab 48
  Purpose tab 46
  Request tab 45
  Schedule tab 50
Amazon Web Services (AWS) 3
Application Programming Interfaces (APIs)
  about 139
  Representational State Transfer (REST)
    API 139
  SOAP APIs 145
  supported APIs 139
Automate workflows
  invoking, ways 82, 83

B

benefits, Red Hat CloudForms 8
bottlenecks
  viewing 137

C

capabilities, Red Hat CloudForms
  about 7
  automate 7
  control 7
  insight 7
  integrate 7
catalogs 52
Ceilometer service
  URL 131
chargeback
  prerequisite 121
  rate, assigning 122
  rate, creating 122
  report, creating 123
  working, with rates 122
charts
  about 132
  capacity and utilization charts,
    viewing 133, 134
CloudForms Management Engine
    Automate model
  about 69
  class, copying 75
  class, creating 74
  custom domain, creating 72
  domains 70
  instance, adding 77, 78
  instance, copying 78, 79
  namespace, creating 73
  namespaces 70
  organizational units 70
  schema, creating 76
  working with 71

J

JavaScript Object Notation (JSON) 140

L

life cycle management
about 53
provisioning 53
retirement 53

M

ManageIQ
about 10
URL 10
methods
about 80
creating 81, 82
global variable ($evm) 80
hierarchy 80
list, URL 80

N

namespaces, CloudForms Management
Engine Automate model
cloud namespace 70
control namespace 71
infrastructure namespace 70
service namespace 71
system namespace 71
namespaces, RedHat
cloud 71
infrastructure 71
integration 71
portfolio 71
system 71

O

OpenStack instance
provisioning 51
Open Virtualization Format (OVF) 6
optimization
Red Hat CloudForms 129

P

policies
about 86
compliance policy 96
control policy 89
simulating 100
types 88
use cases 86
PostgreSQL database
URL 19
prerequisites, data collection
about 130
Red Hat Enterprise Linux OpenStack
platform 131
Red Hat Enterprise virtualization 131
provider information
editing 33-35
viewing 33-35
provisioning
about 42
Amazon EC2 instance 43, 44
types 9
provisioning dialogs
creating 39
customizing 39
structure 38, 39
working with 37
provisioning, types
hosts 9
instances 9
virtual machines 9
ProvisionRequestApproval 54
ProvisionRequestQuotaVerification state
machine 66

Q

quotas
about 66, 67
modifying 67

R

Red Hat CloudForms
about 5
advantages 5

Thank you for buying
Hybrid Cloud Management with
Red Hat CloudForms

About Packt Publishing

Packt, pronounced 'packed', published its first book, *Mastering phpMyAdmin for Effective MySQL Management*, in April 2004, and subsequently continued to specialize in publishing highly focused books on specific technologies and solutions.

Our books and publications share the experiences of your fellow IT professionals in adapting and customizing today's systems, applications, and frameworks. Our solution-based books give you the knowledge and power to customize the software and technologies you're using to get the job done. Packt books are more specific and less general than the IT books you have seen in the past. Our unique business model allows us to bring you more focused information, giving you more of what you need to know, and less of what you don't.

Packt is a modern yet unique publishing company that focuses on producing quality, cutting-edge books for communities of developers, administrators, and newbies alike. For more information, please visit our website at www.packtpub.com.

About Packt Open Source

In 2010, Packt launched two new brands, Packt Open Source and Packt Enterprise, in order to continue its focus on specialization. This book is part of the Packt Open Source brand, home to books published on software built around open source licenses, and offering information to anybody from advanced developers to budding web designers. The Open Source brand also runs Packt's Open Source Royalty Scheme, by which Packt gives a royalty to each open source project about whose software a book is sold.

Writing for Packt

We welcome all inquiries from people who are interested in authoring. Book proposals should be sent to author@packtpub.com. If your book idea is still at an early stage and you would like to discuss it first before writing a formal book proposal, then please contact us; one of our commissioning editors will get in touch with you.

We're not just looking for published authors; if you have strong technical skills but no writing experience, our experienced editors can help you develop a writing career, or simply get some additional reward for your expertise.

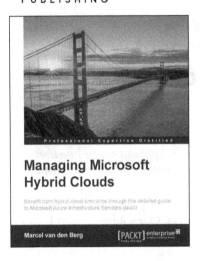
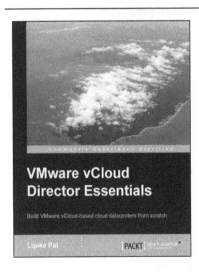

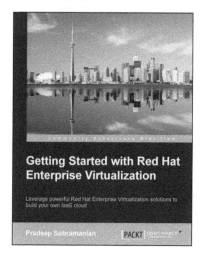
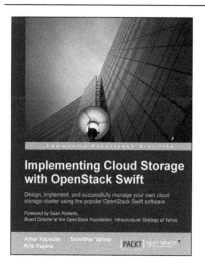